Foreword,

If you're reading this book, you probably already think you able to identify each of the subjects of Carl's pictures by si̱   ⸺ ⸺⸻⸺. but the joy of Carl's photographs is that they make you get to know birds really, really well, in a way that few other nature books do.

Do you know what the underside of a blue tit's feet look like? Or what a bearded tit looks like mid-flight? Or how much of a thug the cute little robin red-breast can be? A lot of people can point an expensive camera and lens at a bird and get a passable result, but very few have the skill and the patience to capture its character. The joyful greed of the puffin with its beak just crammed with fish, the side-eye glance of a stonechat as it comes into land, and the joy of a warbler on a spring day: every page in this book is crammed with true portraits of birds, with the little insight into their lives and personalities that a really spectacular photo gives you.

One of the many beautiful things about this collection is that it isn't just a gallery of rare birds that some of us will never have the time or resources to see. Carl celebrates the little souls that we see or hear every day alongside the glory of a short-eared owl or a phalarope. That's what a true love of nature gives you: the ability to find joy in the commonplace as well as the unusual.

Many of us seek solace in naturalism, using long walks or quiet hours in a bird hide to recharge our minds and souls. But for those evenings when it is too dark and cold to make out more than the outline of a dozing bird, or those days when a miserable fog just won't lift, this book will help you take flight into the colourful world around us.

Words of praise

"I have been following Carl for some time on social media, and his photographs of birds never fail to delight and surprise. I am so pleased that he has been persuaded to gather together some of these beautiful images for his book '100 Birds'. The result is a triumph - a stunning and varied collection of images, paired with charming, informative, insightful, and often humorous, stories. I love it!"

Brigit Strawbridge Howard, Environmentalist and author

"Carl's sheer passion for the natural world around us and his continued efforts to communicate wildlife through photography is truly admirable. His work focussed on UK wildlife, in particular our superb bird species, has engaged thousands of people over the years. This book is not only recognition to his brilliant skills and patience as a photographer, but also something to be shared and enjoyed by all generations of wildlife enthusiasts. And I personally look forward to following his work for many years to come."

Hannah Stitfall, Wildlife presenter

"Carl's stunning photos are full of both charm and vivid drama - he takes 'ordinary' garden birds and turns them into stars!"

Lissa Evans, Novelist and TV director and producer

"From his stunning and impeccably timed captures Carl now takes us on a surreal journey of discovery in which he perfectly encapsulates his passion for photography, the true beauty of nature, and the world's most beautiful birds."

Suzi Mann, Radio and TV presenter

"There are nature photographers, and then there is Carl Bovis. I know of no-one else who is able to capture and bring out the character of Britain's diverse wildlife. His passion for nature pours out of every page, shining a new light on the birds with whom we share the country."

Charlie Taylor, BBC Somerset presenter

"The energy, immediacy and detail of Carl's exquisite photographs will entrance everyone from seasoned birdwatcher to casual observer. Some of the very finest nature photography around."

Simon Blackwell, Comedy writer and producer

"The thing I love most about Carl's photography is the intricate detail. His photos of birds in flight are particularly stunning, especially seeing the wings close up. I don't know how he does it!"

Jenna Myles, Best newcomer at the National Community Radio Awards 2019

"Carl's work is pure joy; a passionate celebration of a class of wildlife I never had much interest in before it popped up on my Twitter timeline. Now I'd be lost without my regular dose of birdy beauty."

Nick Murphy, BAFTA winning director and writer

"I've been following Carl on Twitter for a while now, he is full of positivity and his bird photos are so beautiful. This book is a pleasure for everyone who loves nature."

Tanita Tikaram, Singer-songwriter

I've always had a deep love of nature, and in particular, birds. Being brought up on a fruit farm in the Kent countryside definitely had a lot to do with it. My grandad would delight in showing me where birds were nesting around the farmhouse, and his enthusiasm, along with the curiosity of early childhood, immediately sparked my interest. Every new bird that flew into the garden caught my eye, just as each new birdsong caught my ear. I can vividly remember a spotted flycatcher nest under the guttering of an old brick shed, and also my amazement at a globe-shaped wren's nest, built in the middle of a round coil of hosepipe, hanging from one of the farm building's walls!

Much of my early childhood free time was spent outside, binoculars in hand, eager for the next bird sighting; my interest never waning but growing. To this day I'm still happiest when I'm out and about in nature, enjoying the sights and sounds of the British countryside.

Now living on the beautiful Somerset Levels, I'm lucky enough to see all kinds of birds, every single day. In 2006, my trusty binoculars were replaced by a DSLR camera, and my love for our feathered friends took on a new meaning. Now, not only could I see the birds, I could also photograph them for posterity! All of the photographs I take now still hearken back to those early days on the family farm in Kent. I still get the same sense of wonder and excitement looking through the lens of my camera today as that little boy did all those years ago seeing those birds for the first time. A childhood interest which became a lifelong passion.

This book features 100 of my best, or most interesting, bird photos. Each picture includes information about the bird, how I got the photo, or just personal recollections or memories linked to the image. It's been a labour of love for me, putting it all together. Now I hope that readers will be inspired to get out and see birds for themselves, to put out food and water for them, to keep their gardens green, with the lawns, trees and bushes that many birds desperately need to thrive.

You can buy my prints, postcards, calendars, canvases and greeting cards by visiting my website at carlbovisnaturephotography. blogspot.com or by following me on Twitter, @carlbovisnature or on Facebook, 'Carl Bovis Nature Photography'.

I'd never seen a puffin until June 2018, when I went to Skomer Island in Pembrokeshire, Wales, for the first time. I was invited along by my friend, Justin Hawkins (Not 'The Darkness' singer), the only caveat being that I had to get myself to his house in Weston Super Mare by 3am! Now I don't do early mornings as a rule, and this was so early it was almost the middle of the night. However, the invite was so exciting I was happy to sacrifice my sleep on this occasion.

The reason for the shockingly early start was clear, you cannot buy tickets to day trip to Skomer. They work on a first come, first served basis, which means the earlier you get there and queue, the better your chances of getting on the island. It's over 170 miles from my home on the Somerset Levels to the crossing point at Martin's Haven, a long way to go to literally miss the boat.

Once on the island, there's only one word that can do it justice; Wow! Obviously the puffins are the big draw, and they were everywhere, flying in from the sea from all angles, like little rainbow-tipped missiles! There also seemed to be an inexhaustible supply of sandeels in the surrounding waters, judging by the impressive beakful each returning puffin carried.

This photo was actually taken after my better lens had given up the ghost just minutes before. (Incredible timing!) I used the shorter 70-300mm Nikon lens and managed to freeze the puffin as it came into land. It's one of the favourite photos that I've ever taken and it quickly became my Twitter profile picture when it was clear that other people loved it too. This photo alone made the ridiculously early start to the day worth it.

Boarding the boat to leave the island, I'd already decided that I'd be back again the following year. For a bird loving nature photographer, you can't get much better than Skomer Island!

Goldfinch

When I was a young lad, goldfinches were a bird of the wider countryside and rarely seen in gardens. Greenfinches and chaffinches were regular visitors to our garden in Kent, but the only times I saw their brightly coloured cousins was during family walks that took us past thistle beds. Goldfinches love feeding on their seeds, hence one old country name for them 'thistle finch'. The sunlight often shone through their wings, giving a flash of the golden stripe that give these charming little birds their name. In fact, the name for a group of goldfinches is a 'charm', relating to their twittering song. How very apt!

Fast forward to 2019, and goldfinches are one of the few bird success stories. They regulary visit garden feeders and have a real love of sunflower hearts. I know this, as they have cost me a fortune in seed the last few years! They always turn up 'mob-handed', never alone, and perch in the surrounding trees before making it down to the feeders once they know the coast is clear.

As with most birds, groups means bickering! Goldfinches are no different and often go head to head in mid-air, scolding each other and rapidly gaining height before breaking away and returning to the feeders or trees.

I've tried to photograph this behaviour many times, but it is extremely difficult to gain focus on both birds, without 'clipping' their wings (bird photographer speak for losing part of a wing out of a shot).

On one occassion I was lucky, and I have to thank my eldest daughter Emily Jane, as it was from her bedroom window that I captured this image, much to her annoyance at the time. She likes to do her artwork on the floor, so I had to pick a route very carefully, between drawings of her creation 'Long the Dragon', scattered like ashes on her carpet.

Of all the wild ducks in the UK, I think the pintail must be my favourite. Part of the reason for this is the fact that they're not as common as the other ducks. Wigeon and teal occur in large numbers in suitable wetland habitats during winter, mallards are familiar to everyone and gadwall are pretty but not a striking duck. The pintail, however, is a beauty! As with most birds, it's the male that has the gorgeous looks and in flight the long, pointed tail feathers that give the bird it's name are more obvious.

It's one of those ducks that birdwatchers always want to see when they visit wetlands in the winter. At Greylake, my local RSPB reserve, it's a real challenge to pinpoint the handful of pintail amongst the hundreds of wigeon and teal. The best chance is when something spooks the wildfowl, such as a bird of prey, and they all take to flight en-masse. One such occasion happened just as I entered the main hide, chaos ensued and I ran to a window with my camera at the ready and immediately saw a small group of pintail approaching. I managed to get this shot of two males as they passed overhead.

This is typical of my knack of being in the right place at the right time when it comes to birds. I once went to see a peregrine falcon at the Avon Gorge near Bristol. On arriving at the clifftop viewing point I was greeted by a few familiar faces. 'Are we glad that you're here, Carl,' said one of the disgruntled birders, 'We've been stood here for hours and not had a single sighting, it's bound to come out now!'. Sure enough, within a couple of minutes of my arrival the peregrine put on a bit of a show right in front of us!

I've always been fascinated in the flight of a bird. This ability to rise above the earth and go wherever their wings take them is truly magical and quite miraculous, at least in my mind! I was recently asked by BBC Somerset radio to come into their studio and talk about 'The Big Garden Birdwatch', an annual event organised by the Royal Society for the Protection of Birds, to help decipher the health of garden bird populations in the UK. I was let into the BBC building by someone I recognised, who kindly went and made me a cup of tea whilst I waited to go into the studio. Whilst I sat nervously wondering what I was going to say, I noticed a poster on the wall of all the station's presenters. The guy who had let me in was Simon Parkin, a popular children's TV presenter from the 80s!

Once called into the studio, I took my seat, put on my headphones, and was almost caught out straight away with the opening question; 'So what is it about birds that you particularly love?'

After a pause, I said 'Well, the fact that they can fly, for a start.'

Afterwards, people who had listened to the interview ribbed me mercilessly about the answer I had given, however, the remarkable ability to fly is taken for granted. Humans still haven't invented anything that can get close to the dexterity, effortlessness or beauty of a birds' flight, despite the huge amount of technology now at our disposal.

Capturing birds in flight is the ultimate challenge in bird photography, especially small birds. In recent winters I have taken myself to RSPB Greylake to try and photograph the finches, sparrows and tits that come to the car parks bird tables and feeders. My social media followers are well aware by now of this particular passion in my bird photography, and these in-flight photos are usually quite popular as they capture seldom seen split second mid-air moments and poses.

I loved this photo of a great tit, rounded wings open, legs tucked in, tail spread. It's impossible for me to look at pictures like this and not marvel at the beauty and untouchable natural engineering of a birds' wings and feathers. Indeed, I love birds, because birds can fly!

Whitethroat

The whitethroat is one of my favourite summer visitors, a warbler of thick hedgerows, their scratchy song is a familiar sound of the British countryside. However, as with most warblers, they're easier to hear than see, as they spend much of the time skulking out of sight. Before breeding they perform regular brief song flights, so springtime is probably the best time to get a decent view.

Whitethroats are on the amber list in the UK, they have struggled to recover from a terrible population crash between 1968 and 1969, when numbers arriving on our shores from their West African wintering grounds were 70% down on the previous year! This was mostly blamed on a severe drought, south of the Sahara Desert.

My first experience of a whitethroat was a very sad one. I hadn't been a qualified driver for long, and after a trip in a work van through the Somerset countryside on a beautiful summer's day, I returned to the yard to find a little dead bird stuck in the vans front grill. Of course it was a whitethroat, and I was distraught! The bird must have flown unseen out of a hedge in front of me as I drove down a narrow country lane. I was blameless, it was an unfortunate accident, yet I still felt terrible guilt.

On a much happier note, I managed this photo one spring morning at RSPB Ham Wall, the whitethroat had obviously only recently arrived and was singing away in clear view, not at all worried by the group of people standing and watching it. As I took this photo, Mike Dilger, the BBC wildlife presenter, walked over and asked what I had been photographing. 'A whitethroat' I replied.

'Sounds like a willow warbler actually' he responded. I ended up showing him this image on the back of my camera, to prove that it had indeed been a whitethroat, and just to confirm, the bird helpfully popped back out into view again, still in full voice, whilst Mike was stood beside me. It's quite comforting to know that even the experts get it wrong occasionally!

House Sparrow

House sparrows are one of those birds that everyone is familiar with; however, few people realise that they're actually on the red list of species, meaning they're of most conservation concern. There are still millions, but overall numbers have decreased at an alarming rate in the last 25 years.

I remember a colony living around the bungalow on my family farm on the Somerset Levels years ago. One day, I was suddenly aware that there was none of the usual constant chirping outside. On investigation, I couldn't find a single sparrow! Where had they all gone?

At RSPB Greylake there used to be the odd individual most winters around the car park feeders, but in the last couple of years a decent sized colony had built up, no doubt helped by the regular food supply put out. A reversal of fortune, at this site at least.

This photo of a female was taken as she came down to feed. There's a tiny window of opportunity to get a shot, and it's always a thrill to 'freeze' them as they approach.

I hope this colony continues to thrive at Greylake, and the overall decreasing population trend soon halts. They're delightful birds!

It's a different story in the USA and Canada, however. 200 years ago there were no house sparrows in North America, but after a series of introductions in the mid 1800s, their numbers started to grow rapidly, and there are now an estimated 150 million birds across 48 States! This is bad news for America's native birds, as house sparrows use the same nest sites and are very territorial and more powerful than their rivals, and often destroy the eggs and nestlings of other birds, and even kill the adults! Eastern bluebirds are one particular native species that suffer at the beak of the humble house sparrow, meaning that they're not popular at all with many bird lovers stateside.

Starling

One of my earliest bird memories was on my grandad's fruit farm in Kent, where I grew up. One autumn evening a huge murmuration of starlings passed right over the farmyard and the sky turned black. It was like Armaggedon! For as far as I could see there were birds, making a lot of noise and splattering the yard with droppings! I was open-mouthed with wonder, which probably wasn't the wisest move considering what was falling out of the sky! The starlings settled into the apple orchards, still chattering to one another.

I'd never seen so many birds in one place before that and I was mesmerised by the whole experience.

Now I'm lucky enough to live on the Somerset Levels, which host the biggest starling murmurations in the UK. Up to a million individuals descend on RSPB Ham Wall and Shapwick Heath and it's one of the greatest natural events in Britain. Hundreds of people visit just before dusk during the autumn and winter months to witness it. The big car park quickly fills up, as does the Shapwick Heath one on the opposite side of the road, and visitors have to resort to parking along the narrow lanes outside the reserves. Luckily, there are no double yellow lines or traffic wardens out in 'the sticks' on the Levels! The murmuration has featured on BBC Springwatch and a host of other topical news and nature shows and it really is a sight (and sound) to behold.

Another starling memory concerns a close encounter at my family's bungalow in Somerset. I saw a distressed bird squawking away in the guttering, it looked like it had its leg caught. I quickly grabbed a ladder and climbed up to rescue the stricken starling. I lifted a roof tile beside it and was dumbfounded to see what had actually caught its leg. A rat! I think the rat was just as surprised to see me, because it immediately disappeared back into the roof cavity, letting go of the starling as it did so.

This photo was taken at RSPB Greylake. It's a mini-murmuration of one bird. Just imagine what a million look like! I love the almost symmetrical appearance of its wings and tail as it comes in to land. Just another photo that confirms in my mind what wonderful creatures birds are!

Kestrel

Holywell Bay in Cornwall has always been a magical place for me and holds many wonderful memories of my childhood. My dad would drive my mum, my two sisters, Michelle and Melinda, and myself on holiday from our home in Kent, our little caravan hitched up behind offering a place to get our heads down for the night, as we usually stopped off in some country lay-by half way through the journey. On reaching Cornwall, we often stayed at Hendra Caravan Park near Newquay. Holywell Bay was just down the road and was our favourite beach to visit during our stay.

Wild and beautiful, it had the biggest sand dunes I'd ever seen. When the rest of the family went paddling or surfing in the sea, I grabbed my binoculars and went off birdwatching on my own over the dunes. I saw my first ever common sandpiper here, plus my first ever wheatear and sedge warbler.

One particularly embarrassing time, I clambered over a dune and jumped into a secluded dip, just missing a couple who were wearing very little (as in nothing at all!) and getting to know each other very very well indeed! I couldn't clamber back out again quick enough!

One bird that I used to see regularly was a kestrel, hovering in the sea-breeze by the cliffs. My dad called them 'hawks', so that's what I knew them as when I was young, until I learnt that they were not actually hawks at all, but falcons.

When I returned in 2019 with my own family, there were still kestrels in the exact same spot. I got this photo of a male just after it had finished mating with a female on the cliff-edge. It seems Holywell Bay itself is an aphrodisiac for both man and feathered beast!

Blue Tit

'Blue Tit Feet' was one of those photos that caught the imagination of my Twitter followers, much to my surprise. In the past I would probably have reached for the 'delete' button before even downloading the photo onto my computer, however I was fascinated by the tiny little pads on the bottom of the tit's feet as it flew away. I'd never noticed this before and I was lucky to capture them here with such clarity!

The photo was taken at RSPB Greylake, like many of my little birds in flight photos, and it quickly proved to be one of my most popular shots, with almost 6000 likes on Twitter, one even coming from the infamous politician George Galloway! George once impersonated a cat on the popular reality TV show 'Celebrity Big Brother', so it's possible he just saw the blue tit as food.

After the surprising success of this picture, I looked through my vast back catalogue of bird photos to see if I'd taken similar images in the past. Alas, I found very few, I most likely deleted them all with barely a second glance, but they would not have been as detailed or as dynamic as this picture. I think all nature photographers become obsessed with capturing the 'perfect' photo, to a lesser or greater degree, but in reality, the perfect photo doesn't exist. A better word to strive for is 'unique'. There are so many bird photographers out there now, that capturing something different is increasingly difficult.

'Blue Tit feet' is something a little different, and I think that's why it did so well. I doubt I'll ever capture anything quite like it again!

Blackbird

Blackbirds are one of my favourite garden birds. They are a true thrush, the most common in the UK, and are extremely territorial, the males can often be seen fighting with each other, especially during the breeding season. In fact, their famously gorgeous flutey song is often a proclamation to other males, 'This is my domain, keep away!'.

I will always recall part of my childhood in a country cottage in Kent, laying in my bed as the light faded, listening to the blackbird's 'chink chink chink' alarm calls before they settled down to roost for the night. Such an evocative sound! Shut my eyes and I'm instantly transported back to those simple, beautiful days. We didn't have much, but we lived in the Kent countryside with nature all around us, so in that respect, we were rich indeed.

This photo was taken in my Somerset garden. It shows a squabbling male and female. My guess is that the male wanted to breed and the female wasn't so keen! I saw them flying up from a neighbour's shed roof, then coming down again, out of sight. This happened a few times, so I went indoors to grab my camera, despite being certain that the interaction would cease once I had it in my hands, as 'Sod's law' often dictates. Luckily the action actually carried on for a little while longer, and I was able to capture this mid-air moment, because I was ready and waiting!

It was one of my first photos to earn a 'Notable' award on the 'Bird Guides' website, which I was very proud of, as the quality of the competition there is very high. It was also the photo that encouraged me to try and get more pictures of bird interactions. A very tough photographic quest, but ultimately a very rewarding one.

Sedge Warbler

This is a sedge warbler gripping a reed stem shortly after arriving at RSPB Greylake from its African wintering grounds. Like most warblers, it's more often heard than seen, spending most of its time foraging about in reeds and vegetation. This photo was taken early in the spring which is the best time to get a decent view of them as the males often sing from higher in the reeds and perform regular song flights to attract females. Once they have a mate, the song flights stop and the birds become less visible as they concentrate on nest building and breeding.

My first ever sedge warbler was seen at Holywell Bay in Cornwall when I was a young lad. I still remember the moment vividly. A peaceful, shallow winding river snaked its way past the car park and down to the beach and open sea. My sisters and I would sit in an inflatable boat and my parents would walk in the water, pulling us along.

I always had my binoculars with me, and one day, just before getting into the boat, I heard a warbler's chattering song coming from a reedbed the other side of the river, but was unsure of what species it was. A quick scan of the area with my binoculars revealed nothing at first, but then they fell onto a sparrow sized bird singing away at the top of the reeds, its pale supercilium (stripe above the eye) clearly identifying it as a sedge warbler, as opposed to a reed warbler, which lacks this distinctive stripe.

This first sighting of quite a common summer visitor made my entire holiday! That's the power of nature. My second ever view of a sedge warbler came years later and was quite remarkable, as it was in the family kitchen on the Somerset Levels!

We always used to leave the front door open in our farmland bungalow, and one day my mum came in from the yard and called to me, saying there was a bird in the window, trying to get out. I ran in expecting to find a sparrow or starling, that lived on and around the building, but instead found the warbler, looking all forelorn, until I opened the window and it flew out to freedom.

I am often amazed by the amount of people who claim that they have never seen a wren. This bird may be tiny and rather non-descript, but it's also Britain's most common breeding bird, and has an extremely loud song for such a little creature!

I think some people are just not 'tuned in' to the wildlife around them, so are not paying attention. Wrens can be easily overlooked, as they're always on the move searching for bugs and spiders, which make up the main part of their diet. They're mostly solitary birds, although they have been known to cuddle up together for warmth during cold winter nights, in tree holes or nest boxes, with up to 60 birds recorded entering a single box!

They feature prominently in folklore, and are referred to as 'King bird' in some parts of the world thanks to the famous Aesop fable about a wren outwitting a magnificent eagle by hitching a ride on the its back then launching off and flying higher once the eagle tired, thus proving that sheer size and strength alone were no match for cleverness.

In the Middle Ages, it was common practice to give birds personal names. Some went on to become their regular common names as used today, such as the 'Mag-pie' and the 'Jack-daw', and some are often referred to with a nickname, hence why the wren is unofficially known as the 'Jenny wren'.

Having said all this, wrens are far from easy to photograph, due to their habit of staying quite low to the ground and rarely stopping for more than a second or two, unless it's to belt out their distinctive song. For this shot, I was at Brean Down Cove in Somerset, sat on rocks waiting for a rare black redstart to show itself, when a wren, which had been feasting on flies in the seaweed, hopped up onto a stick just ten feet in front of me! The result was an unusually close and clear photo of a wren, in good light, with a pleasing clean background. I couldn't believe my luck!

One of the birds that I love to capture in flight at RSPB Greylake is the chaffinch. I often leave seed on a post for them to eat, and they will usually hover for a second or two before landing. I'm not sure why they do this, maybe they're just making sure that it's safe to land. I'm glad that they do it though, because it gives me a better opportunity to photograph them in flight!

I called this photo 'Angelic Chaffinch' for obvious reasons. These wings will have been in this perfect position for literally less than a thousandth of a second, so setting a fast shutter speed on the camera was a must. It's almost impossible to get a shot like this on an 'auto' setting, as there is no way of telling the camera what you are photographing, and it will take everything into consideration, especially the available light, before setting the shutter speed. Invariably, even in good light, the camera will set a slower shutter speed than is required to 'freeze' a little bird in flight.

I was asked to display some of my nature pictures in frames on the walls of a popular country restaurant, 'Clavelshay Barn' near North Petherton in Somerset, by the lovely owner Sue Milverton, and this was one of the photos I chose. Now all the diners are 'watched' by my birds as they tuck into the Barn's famously delicious local cuisine. It's quite ironic that this angelic chaffinch was photographed hovering above food, as now it is hovering above food permanently!

As a thank you, Sue invited me to an early morning 'Dawn chorus' walk on the Quantock Hills beside her restaurant with a group of nature loving people, including talented local artist Jackie Curtis, whom I had not met before, but had long admired her work, as we'd followed each other on social media for years. Talking of 'following', at one stage of the walk, I was followed across a field by a group of sheep. I felt like the 'Pied Piper'! Jackie photographed the scene for posterity and posted the pic on Twitter. We got back to the Barn having heard and seen many birds and Sue made everyone a delicious breakfast. Such a pleasant weekend morning, it made a change to laying in until 10am..

Stonechat

Like many birds, the stonechat gets its name from its call, which sounds like two stones being tapped together. It is often uttered from the top of a bush on heaths and coastal areas. These birds like to sit out in the open, and are not a skulking species like some small birds are, particularly warblers, so you have a good chance of seeing one if you visit suitable habitat, especially in the winter.

The bird in this photo is a female, and as is the general rule in the avian world, she has a more drab plumage than the handsome male. The reason for this is down to courtship and the different roles the sexes undertake. Males compete to earn the right to breed. This isn't done in battle, although of course fights between all male bird species can break out during the breeding season and the lead up to it. Other ways males compete for the female's attention is through their songs and their plumage. The brighter, cleaner and more complete breeding plumage is more attractive to a female as it indicates a strong and healthy male; and consequently, good genes for her offspring.

One of my favourite spots to photograph stonechats is on the heathy common land behind the sand dunes of Woolacombe Beach in North Devon. Whilst my family are playing in the surf and on the sand, I'm usually stalking this area with my camera looking for birds. Not only is it good for stonechats, it's also a great place to see linnets, whitethroats, wheatears and kestrels.

I didn't take this picture at Woolacombe though, it was shot at Steart Marshes, a reasonably new Wildfowl and Wetlands Trust reserve on the coast near Hinkley Point nuclear power station in Somerset. She had been sitting on the top of the branch and briefly flew off in pursuit of a fly before returning again. I have a photo somewhere of me capturing this shot, taken by my middle daughter Erin Louise. I thought that you'd probably prefer to see this one.

Short Eared Owl

Like many people, I've always had a fascination with owls. This is mostly due to their round, human-like faces, their intense stare and mostly nocturnal habits. Much of the fascination could also be attributed to the place of the owl in myth, legend and folklore. The image of the 'wise old owl' can be linked back to ancient times, for the owl was the symbol of the Greek goddess Athena (Roman Minerva) goddess of wisdom and war. Athena's owl was even depicted on Athenian drachmas and the coins themselves were commonly referred to as glaukes 'owls'.

My very first short eared owl was seen on the outskirts of my Somerset village back in 2005. Back in those days, digital photography was a fairly new invention and I only had a tiny 'point and shoot' camera. The owl was hunting in a field opposite the village allotments, and a small crowd of locals had gathered to watch it. I didn't even try to photograph it until it landed. It was about 100 metres away, and the resulting photo was just of a tiny vague blob on a post!

One guy next to me had a DSLR with a huge lens on it. He'd photographed the owl in flight, coming straight for him and showed me the image on the back of his camera. My mouth fell open in shock. 'Wow', I mouthed in wonder at this incredibly detailed and sharp capture. It was at that moment that I decided to buy a DSLR myself.

It wasn't until 2019 that I managed to get a decent 'short eared owl on a post' shot. This photo came about like many of my pictures do, just by being in the right place at the right time! I'd driven to Steart Marshes in the hope of seeing a hunting owl, and as I crawled down the main road through the reserve (in my van, not on my hands and knees), I noticed the owl, sat on a post on the verge! In almost panic, I grabbed my camera, which was on the passenger seat and lowered the window, praying the shortie wouldn't immediately fly off like a buzzard would do! Luckily the owl was unconcerned by my presence, and sat there posing nicely whilst I rattled off a few shots, counting my blessings as I did so. Magic!

Rook

Rooks are highly gregarious members of the crow family. They're common throughout the UK, especially on agricultural land but often get confused with the similar carrion crow. The best way to tell them apart is that rooks have a pale patch on their faces at the base of their beaks, whereas the carrion crow's face is all black. Another identifying feature is the fact that rooks are usually seen together in loose flocks, both large and small, and even nest together in noisy rookeries in the tops of tall trees. Carrion crows are normally only seen in ones and twos.

Having said all this, the rook in the photo was actually on its own! It had come down to have a drink from a puddle, close to where I was parked next to the beach at Blue Anchor, near Minehead in Somerset. After quenching its thirst, it hopped up onto a fence post and sat there contemplating the world around it. I started up my vehicle and crept a little closer, turning the wheel slightly to the left to give myself a clear view out of the driver's window to get a picture. I've found to my cost in the past that you can't take photos through the front windscreen, the slope of the glass distorts the image.

After having a bit of a scratch and a preen, it settled down on the post and turned its head to look straight at me, as if begging me to take its picture. Of course, I duly obliged, and shortly after, it flew off to join its rook mates in a neighbouring field.

The collective term for a group of rooks is called a 'Parliament'. This refers to rooks being seen to form circles around an individual as if putting it on trial. There have been various accounts in history of the bird in the centre being attacked by the ones on the outside, seemingly finding it guilty of whatever heinous corvid crime it was accused of!

Kestrel

Brean Down is one of my favourite places in Somerset. It's a promontory that extends one and a half miles into the Bristol Channel and rises to a height of almost 330 feet in places. It's a fantastic place to walk, with stunning views in all directions, looking across the sea to the islands of Flat Holm and Steep Holm, with the Welsh coast further on, all easily visible on a clear day. To the South lays the six mile stretch of sand and mudflats, taking in Brean Beach, Berrow flats and Burnham on Sea. To the North is the popular, bustling resort of Weston Super Mare.

During one particular visit with my family, I saw a male kestrel above my head. He flew over the fort at the far end of the Down, before dropping down the other side of a cliff. 'It's landed!' I said to myself and quickly made my way over to the area where it had disappeared from view. Gingerly peering over the cliff edge, I could see no sight of the falcon. I stepped up onto two rocks, a foot on each one, and briefly breathed in the sea air. Then I noticed movement right below me. I looked down between my feet, only to be met by the piercing stare of the kestrel, no more than two metres away on a little grassy slope! I slowly brought my camera up to photograph it, but I couldn't focus, as the bird was too close for my zoom lens to focus on correctly, I was worried he would fly away and I'd be left with a close encounter of the blurred kind!

I only got this shot after standing on tip-toes, getting just the right distance from the subject to acquire focus, whilst being buffeted by the strong sea breeze in this exposed spot! The kestrel was unperturbed. It had a stretch, seemed to yawn and peered out to sea, even letting me point it out to my partner and daughters, who had all walked over, curious to see what I had been photographing, before it finally took off and disappeared further along the headland. My family were just as amazed as I was at this magical close encounter with a wild bird of prey. It's not something that happens very often!

Chew Valley Lake in North Somerset is the fifth largest artificial lake in the UK, and a great area for birds with over 260 species recorded since it was opened by The Queen in the early 1950s.

Unfortunately, I rarely have the time to explore the area properly, but there are a couple of places where main roads pass right alongside the water, and these have long laybys for people to stop and enjoy the views and birds. One of those places is known as Herriot's Bridge, somewhere I first stopped 20 years ago in a forlorn hope of seeing an extremely rare booted eagle with my partner Nicola, who was heavily pregnant with our first daughter, Emily Jane, at the time.

During one short stop in 2015, I walked across the road to say hello to a fellow birder that I recognised. He had a telescope pointing in the direction of the muddy water's edge, looking for wading birds. I leant on the stone bridge and looked down to see a shoal of fish. The sun was right above my head, meaning I could see into the water clearly. All of a sudden, a great crested grebe came swimming in at great speed, underneath the water, and scattered the fish in all directions. I'd never seen anything like it!

The fish stayed under the bridge, which offered shade, and the great crested grebe kept coming up and then diving down again on the attack. This went on for about 20 minutes, during which I grabbed my camera and tried to capture the action, but it was very difficult tracking the fast moving grebe under the water and focusing, especially as there was only a small area with clear visibility, and I needed the grebe to come into it. Luckily, that is exactly what happened, and I got this shot of it homing in on its unfortunate prey!

It was a very exciting few minutes, and a thrill to witness.

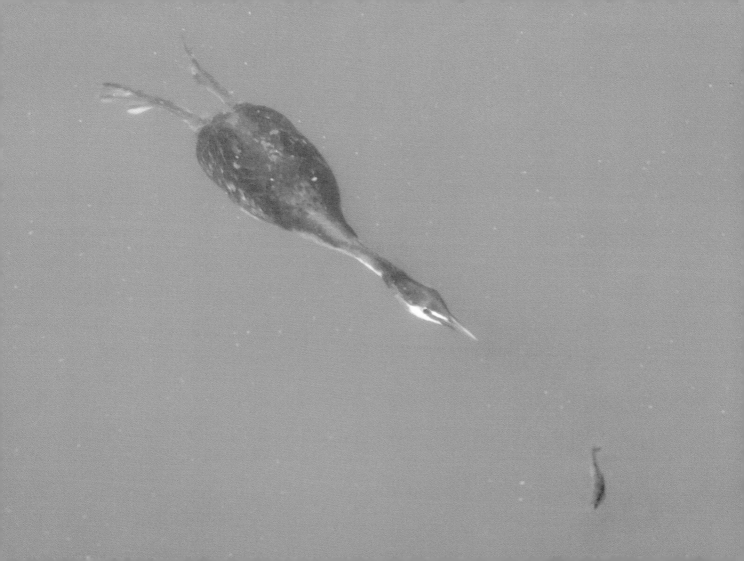

I take pride in trying to get the best photos I can, technically good, sharp, great lighting and composition etc etc, it's a real challenge trying to get pictures that I deem good enough to share on my Facebook nature page and Twitter accounts.

During one extremely dark and miserable winter day in Somerset, I didn't even bother taking my camera out of the house, instead, I put out some bird food, topped up the bird bath (actually a plant pot base), then settled down to take a few snaps through the kitchen window of birds coming into the garden.

High ISOs combined with slower shutter speeds and a gloomy garden meant quite 'noisy' and dark photos, and I didn't have any intention of sharing the pics on my social media sites. However, the weather remained miserable for a number of days after, and as I didn't have anything new to share I reluctantly decided to post one of the pictures, a robin having a bath. I'd taken a series of shots as it splashed about and I couldn't decide which one to share. I asked my other half for her opinion, and she immediately pointed to this picture. 'Now, that's a lovely photo!' she said.

To my total surprise, as soon as I posted it on my Facebook page, the likes, comments and shares immediately took off, with quite a few people proclaiming it the cutest robin photo they had ever seen!

Since then, I've sold many prints of this pic, and have also recently put it on postcards and greeting cards, and it remains as popular as ever. Which just goes to show, photographic perfection is not the be all and end all, sometimes you just need to point your camera out of your kitchen window on a dark and gloomy day and capture something quite cute!

Albino House Sparrow

One summer day in 2018, my eight year old daughter, Skye Rose, told me about a strange white sparrow that she'd seen whilst walking home from the village allotments with her mum, and a couple of days later I received a Facebook message from a village resident who also claimed to have seen it. So that evening, after I'd finished work, I took my camera along to the area where it had been seen and kept my fingers crossed. There was a colony of sparrows chirping away in the thick brambles and bushes, but I didn't see the rare bird at first. Just as the light started fading, a female house sparrow came out into the open, closely followed by her strikingly different offspring, begging to be fed. It really was a case of being 'all white' on the night! I was able to grab a few shots before making my way home, feeling very happy.

That evening, BBC Springwatch shared my pictures of the sparrow on their Twitter account saying it was probably a leucistic bird istead of the much rarer albino. However, I went to photograph it again the following night, in better light, and the resulting photo clearly showed the pink eyes of a true albino! Chris Packham shared my pic on his Twitter page, basically confirming it, and after that, everything went a bit crazy!

I was contacted by news agencies, and within a day, my photos of the young albino were in local and national newspapers, both online and in print, and shown on the local ITV news. I also gave my first ever radio interview, to BBC Somerset, which was so far out of my comfort zone that I insisted it had to be a pre-recorded interview instead of a live one, so that they could edit out all the mistakes I would inevitably make. As it was, I surprised myself by not messing up very many times at all.

The following day, the story had spread around the world! They say everyone has their 15 minutes of fame, and this was clearly mine.

When you look at the back of the camera and see that you've managed to 'freeze' an action shot of a small bird with sharp detail, the buzz is incredible. People never see small birds frozen in time like this usually, as all the action happens in the blink of an eye. I have some techniques I use to try and photograph them, and I hone these and adjust them regularly to push myself to improve and get better shots. I'm never truly happy, always wanting to get the 'perfect' shot. It's that forlorn quest that keeps me coming back. Small common birds may bore some people after a while, but I never tire of them, and always strive to photograph them in different ways and poses. Getting in-flight interaction between small birds is extremely difficult. The amount of things that can go against your chances of getting a good shot are too numerous to list!

The humble robin is probably the fiercest of the little birds in the garden. They are very territorial and will not tolerate other small birds or other robins in their space, especially if there's a food source nearby!

The robin in this picture was again at RSPB Greylake. If another small bird came to the bird table whilst the robin was on it, it would chase it off aggressively. I love this shot of the robin above the blue tit, hanging in the air like Keanu Reeves in 'The Matrix', before dropping down onto the unfortunate tit to administer a decisive blow! It could be seen as bullying, but this is purely survival. Birds don't do anything 'for effect'. I've heard many people call particular species bad or nasty, but they're trying to put human qualities into wild animals and birds, so that, in their own minds, they can easily dismiss and condemn certain species, such as gulls and crows. I'm always trying to change people's opinions of these unfairly maligned birds.

Luckily the blue tit in the photo was unharmed, and was soon back on the table, risking the moody robin's wrath once again.

Black Redstart

Sometimes, a bit of bad news can lead to some unexpected good news. One such example occurred when something happened that brings all nature photographers out in a cold sweat. My lens developed a major fault.

It was the Sigma 150-600mm Contemporary lens, the one I'd been using for all my nature and bird photos for the previous two and a half years. For some reason it had decided to stop focusing on my Nikon D500, and the vibration reduction was also messing about. So I had to go back to using my old cheap Nikon 70-300mm VR lens for a while.

Now, whilst this was a major disappointment, it did have its up side too. I'd forgotten what a delightful lens the 70-300mm is to use. Obviously it didn't have the reach of my Sigma 150-600mm, but it was so much smaller and lighter, and if you could get close enough to your subjects you could capture some very nice shots.

Proof of this was when I used it to photograph a beautiful long-staying female black redstart at Brean Down in Somerset. I managed to get this photo, one of my best ever shots, of her in mid-air about to catch a fly. I doubt I would have captured this moment with my heavier and slower Sigma lens!

At the end of 2018, the year in which I took this shot, I ran a series of polls on my Twitter account of the best photos I'd taken during the year, and asked my followers to vote for their favourites. After a few rounds, the photos were whittled down to a final four, and this picture ran out overall winner. Officially my best photo of 2018! Taken with a pretty cheap lens that I'd had for years and longed to upgrade! Be careful what you wish for.

Blue Tit

You are not just looking at any old blue tit. Not all blue tits are made the same, and not all of them wear capes! This is 'Super Tit', gliding in to save the day!

Super Tit rapidly became my most popular photo on Twitter, with over 10,000 'likes' at the time of writing! If any bird deserves to go 'viral', it's surely one that possesses the superpowers other tits can only dream of!

Like many of my little birds in flight photos, this was taken at RSPB Greylake and stayed hidden away on my computer for three or four months until I finally got around to sharing it. Super Tit cannot be held back!

I often come up with little captions or stories around my bird photos when I post them on social media, usually with tongue firmly in cheek. This captures my followers imagination's and the ensuing interactions are always fun. Giving my birds different characters makes them more appealing and memorable.

When I uploaded this shot, I immediately imagined this little dynamo of a tit as a superhero bird, the way its wings were held back like some kind of cape, its trailing tail adding to the illusion. A steely look of determination painted all over his little face further confirmed my thoughts. I gave the photo the caption 'Never fear, Super Tit to the rescue!'

It was only after the photo took off that I kicked myself that I hadn't given it the obvious rhyming caption of 'Never fear, Super Tit is here!' This oversight did not hold Super Tit back however, far from it! I made prints, fridge magnets and even T-shirts emblazoned with him, and many people invited him into their homes as a result, feeling much safer due to his presence. What a hero!

Bearded Tit

The bearded tit is an enchanting, scarce, colourful and elusive little bird exclusively found in extensive reedbeds that confusingly isn't a member of the tit family at all! Superficially, it resembles a long tailed tit, at least in shape and length of tail, so this is probably how it originally got its name, though its alternative name would be a much better fit; the bearded reedling.

Now, as I'm being a little pedantic, I may as well continue further, as the bearded tit doesn't actually have a 'beard' at all, but a 'moustache'.

As in most humans, it's the males not the females that are facially adorned, but the plainer females have an understated beauty themselves. So I suggest that a less misleading name be used for this delightful bird from this moment on:

The moustached reedling.

There, now that's much more accurate!

Anyway, despite living on the Somerset Levels for the last 30 years, amazingly, it wasn't until a couple of years ago that I first saw these charismatic birds.

I saw them at Westhay Moor nature reserve, where the owners, Somerset Wildlife Trust, put grit down on the boardwalk to one of the hides in the reeds, especially for the bearded tits/moustached reedlings. During the summer these birds eat the plentiful insects and feed them to their young, which are high in much needed protein to aid growth. During the autumn and winter, their diet changes to seed, but they struggle to digest them, so need to take on grit to help grind the seeds up.

I was delighted to get this photo of a male in flight after it had briefly perched at the top of a reed stem, before flying down to stock up on the important grit.

Some people say that you shouldn't get too close to a rare bird. When a rarity turns up, such as this delightful grey phalarope, birders naturally want to see it, and bird photographers naturally want to photograph it.

The problems arise due to an unspoken competitiveness amongst some bird photographers. They all want to get the best shot of the rare bird. This is only natural, but we need to keep a number of things in mind.

Firstly, the welfare of the rare bird itself. They are rare for a reason. Usually they have been blown off course during their migration, so are tired, vulnerable and need to feed and rest for a day or 2 to build their strength sufficiently to enable them to go on their way and hopefully reach their initial intended destination.

Secondly, the welfare of any other birds and nature, that could be affected by attempts to photograph the rare bird, including the environment it finds itself in.

Thirdly, we have to think about other birders and nature lovers that would like to come and see and enjoy the bird themselves. Some people come hundreds of miles just to see a rare bird, and you could understand their annoyance if a hapless photographer had scared the bird away; and their time, travel and money spent getting there had all been wasted!

This beauty was at the Huntspill seawall near Burnham on sea, a great place for birds. It was on a tiny pool, there were no other birds around to disturb and it was right beside a footpath. This bird was ridiculously confiding, and an absolute delight to watch as it swam about, constantly picking food/bugs off the surface of the water, its head going up and down rapidly and constantly, a bit like a woodpecker pecking at a tree. At one point, it swam right up to where I was laying, so close that my camera wasn't able to focus on it!

My partner particularly loves this picture, of all the photos I've ever taken, this is her favourite.

Marsh Harrier

This hovering beauty is a marsh harrier, a bird that was extremely rare a couple of decades ago, but now doing really well on the Somerset Levels. I took the photo at Catcott Lows nature reserve. The previous time I'd seen a marsh harrier, I was sharing the back of a car with one! Here's the story.

One morning, whilst I was still lounging in bed, I received a call from my mate Geoff Head. He told me he was at nearby RSPB Greylake and was sitting next to an injured marsh harrier!

He'd been trying to get help for a couple of hours with no luck, but didn't want to leave the bird's side in case further harm came to it. I jumped straight out of bed, and with the help of my other half, Nicola, found a big enough cardboard box to fit the bird in. She taped up the bottom of the box, put some newspaper in and grabbed some towels plus a thick pair of her gardening gloves, then I quickly drove to Greylake to find Geoff and the harrier.

I soon found Geoff crouching down within feet of the beautiful bird of prey, which was laying prone on the grass. Geoff thought she may have a broken leg or a broken wing, but on putting on the gloves and approaching her slowly she stood up OK and spread her wings in a defensive posture, and even lifted a talon to swipe at him!

We decided the only way to safely get hold of her was to throw one of the towels over her and grab her quickly before she struggled and possibly injured herself more. Geoff did this expertly, and I held the box open for him to put her in. One of her talons came through the towel and grabbed one of Geoff's gloved fingers! Bringing the gloves was definitely a good idea!

Geoff then drove to Secret World Wildlife Rescue at nearby East Huntspill, with me in the back of the car holding the box steady. The staff were surprised by their new admission, and it wasn't to be the only time I needed the wonderful help of Secret World that year.

Peregrine Falcon

RSPB Greylake really comes into its own in the winter, as hundreds of wild duck arrive to spend the cold, grey months in the relative safe haven of the reserve. I say 'relative safe haven' because in nature, nowhere is totally safe for wildlife. There will always be predators about, and that's how it should be. As 'The Lion King' and Sir Elton John helpfully pointed out, it's the circle of life!

One such predator is the peregrine falcon. These magnificent birds of prey are the fastest creatures on earth.

The huge amounts of potential prey wintering at Greylake inevitably attract a peregrine or two. One day I managed to capture this photo of a hunting peregrine in mid 'stoop', which I was very happy about, as when they're stooping after prey they can reach speeds of over 200 miles per hour! The ducks had no chance and within seconds an unfortunate teal had been caught and killed in mid-air by this beautiful but deadly hunter. The photo proved very popular on my social media sites, and was also shared by the BBC.

In the last couple of years, a pair of peregrine have set up home on the tower of St Mary Magdalene Church in the nearby County town of Taunton. They have successfully bred too, much to the delight of the local wildlife lovers, and the despair of Taunton's town pigeons. The vicar even raised money for a webcam so that people could watch the progress of the peregrine chicks from the comfort of their own homes. I presume that they will grow up to be birds of pray.

After seeing some of my photos of the falcon pair on his church spire on my Facebook page, he contacted me to ask if he could use some of them on his fundraising website. Of course, I agreed to his request, and enough money was consequently raised for the project to succeed.

No doubt these peregrines will be visiting Greylake over the coming winters, after all, a duck would be a tasty treat after a diet of pigeons!

Hudsonian Godwit

One Saturday morning, something caught my eye as I was surfing Twitter. Apparently, there was a Hudsonian Godwit at Meare Heath on the Somerset Levels, just up the road from where I was working! It was amongst a flock of black tailed godwits, a close relative that is common on the local reserves. The Hudsonian version is a North American species, and had only ever been seen in the UK three times previously, the last time in the early 80s!

In twitching parlance, this was a 'Mega' or a 'Blocker', to everyone else it was a 'very rare bird'. I don't 'twitch' rare birds as such, but if one turns up on my local patch I like to get to see it if I can.

After finishing work, my other half and I made our way to the new RSPB Ham Wall car park, opposite Meare Heath. It was packed! We walked over the road and made our way to the scrape where the star bird had been residing. We passed so many other birders, I'd never seen so many in my life. People had come from as far away as Norfolk and the North of England to see this bird.

Opposite the scrape, a wall of tripods adorned with telescopes and cameras were trained on a group of black tailed godwits. A kindly birder let us have a look through his telescope, and sure enough, there was the Hudsonian, standing out against the 'cleaner' black tails. It wasn't very active, but it was a thrill to see. Shortly after this, it disappeared from view under a bank.

That was that, I thought, and we started to make our way back to the car, when all of a sudden a bird of prey put all the birds up and I fired off a few shots of the flock of godwits as they passed overhead. Luckily, the Hudsonian could be seen clearly, thanks to its black underwing, which all the the other birds in the flock lacked. It's a much darker bird in general, and therefore, much easier to pick out in flight. Not my greatest ever photo, but certainly the rarest bird I'm ever likely to photograph in the UK!

Fieldfare

'The Beast from the East' was coming...

Early March 2018 had me continually reviewing every weather forecast for my area of Somerset, as the prediction of heavy snow had me buzzing with excitement like a little kid.

I love snow, but as a nature lover, my love has some reservations, as I know lots of birds perish in freezing conditions. I took solace in the fact the bad weather was only due to last a couple of days, and I posted on my local Facebook groups reminding people to put out food and water for the birds.

The snow started falling as I was at work. I kept looking out of the office window, wishing I was at home to enjoy this rare event. On the Somerset Levels, snow is unusual, the last winter where snow 'laid' was way back in 2011!

My itch to get home increased further when my other half, Nicola, texted me to say there was a redwing in the garden. I'd only ever seen one in my garden once before, in the 25 years I'd lived there. A few minutes later she texted again, this time to say that there was a fieldfare in the garden. I'd never seen a fieldfare there full stop!

As the snow started to fall harder and an unprecedented red weather warning was issued, my boss finally sent everyone home before the worst of the weather came. I couldn't wait to get home, and rushed into my kitchen and looked out onto our little back garden. Sure enough, there was a fieldfare right in front of my back door, enjoying an apple that my other half had put out. I lay down and pushed my lens through the cat-flap and took this photo.

Judging by social media, I wasn't the only one having fieldfares and redwings in the garden for the first time, people all over Somerset, and all over the UK had them visiting too. This was due to the unusually late timing of the snow. Redwings and fieldfares are winter visitors that feed on berries until the supply in the countryside has been exhausted, then they take to the fields to find food. The snowfall covered the fields, and with the berries all gone, they had no choice but to venture into gardens to feed. I wasn't complaining!

Lesser Whitethroat

One sunny afternoon in mid-summer, I visited RSPB Greylake, knowing full well that birds would be hard to see and photograph as the undergrowth had grown very high, hiding most of them. Birds also moult after breeding, so this is another reason for them to keep out of sight, as the moulting process makes them more vulnerable to predation. However, I was hoping to get some butterflies instead, and luckily there were plenty about, mainly peacocks, red admirals and green-veined whites, which were all enjoying the abundant flowering hemp-agrimony.

It was whilst photographing the insects that I noticed a small patch of undergrowth where small birds were flitting about, occasionally showing briefly on an old dead branch. I stood motionless in one spot for about an hour, and in that time I had repeated views of five or six different warblers, all in the same area! These were reed warbler, sedge warbler, willow warbler, common whitethroat and possibly a young chiffchaff, though this could have been a young willow warbler, as they're very hard to tell apart when they're not singing. It was amazing to see so many different warblers in such a tiny space!

The best warbler sighting by far though was a lesser whitethroat, an uncommon and elusive bird that I'd never seen at Greylake before, and had only ever seen four or five times in my whole life. After getting a brief but decent enough view to confirm what it was, I waited patiently, hoping it would come out into the open so I could get a clear photograph of it. Sure enough, it briefly showed on the old dead branch I mentioned earlier, and I got this shot, with the pinks of the hemp-agrimony adding a pleasing dash of colour. They're rarely seen out in the open, so I was thrilled with this photograph. Patience really does pay off.

Meet Dave.

Poor Dave wanted desperately to be in this book. His apparent sadness in this picture is due to the fact he originally didn't make the cut. I shared his distressing story in a series of tweets on my Twitter page, and my followers soon took poor Dave to their hearts.

Many demanded that Dave be included in the book, even if I had to rename it '101 Birds' to accommodate him!

Here are just some of their comments.

Jayne Nancekivell - 'Oh Dave, what a sad little face. We love you Dave, Keep your beak up!'

Helen Wrigley - 'Poor Dave! Always the bridesmaid...'

Tracey Stanway - 'I hear a chant; We want Dave, we want Dave..'

Jonathan J Stedman - 'Carl, it's bad luck to have 100. More auspicious to have 101. You know it's the right thing to do..'

Melanie Gibney - '#JusticeForDave'

Kathy Degner - 'I love Dave. I want to adopt him. I'm sure he'd love living in Southern California.'

Ella Beard - 'Dave deserves a book of his own! #PoorDave'

Eco Witch - 'Room on the back cover for him perhaps? Poor little fella..'

Arte & Tinta - 'Devastated, you broke his heart! Not fair, what about a little corner on a page?'

Lazy Cuttlefish - 'Team Dave'

After such an outpouring of love for poor Dave the puffin, how could I possibly leave him out of the book?

So here he is. Looking sad, but this was before he earnt himself a legion of loyal fans. Go Dave!

Turtle Dove

One bird that has eluded me all my life is the turtle dove. They were already scarce in the UK when I was a kid growing up in Kent, but they're now even rarer, a sad decline of a delightful little dove.

When I heard that there was a turtle dove giving close views at Northwick Warth, on the banks of the Severn River near Bristol, I couldn't resist calling in on the way past one day to see if I could finally see one, and hopefully get a photo too.

It was quite a dull day, but it was a wonderful place for birding. There were skylarks, linnets, wheatears, pied wagtails and meadow pipits all over the place on the short grass, and in the sheltered pools were flocks of black tailed godwits, redshanks and dunlin, some knot and snipe, plus a single spotted redshank, a bird I'd only ever seen once before.

Alas, the birders present had been there most of the morning and none had seen the turtle dove. I was a bit gutted, I took some photos of a magpie hopping about on the backs of some cattle to console myself, then I started to walk back to my parked car.

Most of the birders had gone by this stage, but as I passed one, he said something which I missed, 'pardon?' I asked.

'Turtle dove' he whispered, pointing to the short grass just below the path we were stood on. Sure enough, there was the elusive dove, slowly and unobtrusively walking about, pecking every now and then at the ground. I must have walked past it and not even noticed! I was struck by how small it seemed compared to its common relative the collared dove, and despite its beautiful colours and markings, it was quite well camouflaged in the grass. The bird was very confiding, I laid down on my stomach on the bank and managed some close shots, without needing to go right up to it and possibly flushing it.

I left very happy that I had finally 'ticked' the bird off my life list, plus managed some decent shots of it to boot!

Lesser Black Back Gull

There is no such thing as a seagull. Look through any field guide to birds and you will not find one. For a long time most gulls lived by the sea, nesting on cliffs and islands and feeding mainly on marine fish and invertebrates, plus other birds and their eggs. Lack of space and dwindling fish stocks coupled with the UK Clean Air Act of 1956, which forbade the burning of refuse at landfill sites, led to gulls moving inland in the search of suitable breeding grounds. Buildings replicated the cliffs that they had traditionally nested on, and thanks to their omnivorous and varied diet, landfill now offered a regular and plentiful food source.

In short, gulls moving inland was caused in the main by human beings. Now many people call gulls 'pests' or 'sky rats'. They're easily the most unpopular group of birds in the UK, not helped by ridiculous scaremongering in the British tabloid media. I actually read a story recently in a national newspaper, that said gulls could easily take a human baby!

Personally, I love gulls. They also need protecting. The herring gull is now on the Red List of threatened UK birds, the highest possible conservation status. Whenever I tell people this, they're usually incredulous, 'but they're everywhere!' they exclaim.

The angry gull in this photo is actually a lesser black backed gull. They used to be irregular in Britain, but now they're more common than their similar cousin. They have dark grey backs and yellow legs. This shot was taken outside the office I work in. Whilst walking from my van to the office, this gull would regularly dive-bomb me, as it had a chick on the office roof. It's not evil or being nasty, it was simply protecting its young from a perceived threat, something we would all do for our children!

Shelduck Chicks

One day in spring 2019, I was driving down a main road in Burnham-on-Sea, going about my regular 9 to 5 job as a traffic surveyor, when I noticed three tiny balls of fluff running down the middle of the road in front of me! I immediately stopped my van and turned my flashing hazard beacons on to prevent traffic from running over the little ducklings, then jumped out to try and shepherd them off the road to safety. They ran off down a track, their little legs a blur, heads turning left and right as if in panic, before disappearing from view around a corner. This was when I took this photo.

That was that I thought. I got back in my van and pulled over to the side of the road and the traffic started flowing again. These were shelduck chicks, and I pondered how they had come to be running down a road in the middle of a busy town in the first place! Of course, Burnham is right on the Somerset coast, the 'on-Sea' part of its name being a bit of a giveaway, but it still seemed a very strange place for them to be!

I was just about to leave when the ducklings suddenly reappeared and ran straight back out into the road again! Once again, I shot out into the traffic, and managed to stop it in both directions. However, the distressed chicks separated, with two of them darting into a garden and the other one running down the road in the opposite direction. I chased after it, keeping the traffic crawling along behind me, and it disappeared down a grassy track. I called Secret World Wildlife Rescue, asking for assistance and two of their volunteers quickly arrived and managed to catch the other pair of ducklings in a net. We tried to find the other chick at the end of the track but had no luck, however we did see an adult shelduck come down in the field behind it, so fingers crossed it was a parent, and that it was reunited with its young.

The story made the local press, and one of my photos appeared in The Times national newspaper. I was just in the right place at the right time.

Whimbrel

Battery Point, at Portishead, juts out into the Bristol Channel and is a good location for purple sandpipers. With this in mind, one afternoon I visited in the hope of seeing these scarce and easily missed little waders. Alas, I did not find any. However, I did happen across a fabulous consolation, a whimbrel on the rocks. These large waders, with long down-curved bills, pass through Somerset on their spring migration, but are not easy to get a close view of. They are easily mistaken for the very similar resident curlew, but they're a bit smaller, their bills aren't quite as long and they have a stripe over the eye that the curlew lacks. These identifying features are not clear from a distance, and it's usually from a distance that these birds are viewed!

The whimbrel that I saw was so camouflaged on the rocks that I didn't notice it at first and inadvertently flushed it. It flew off, around the Point, over the sea and landed in the distance on the beach. I cursed myself, thinking that a great photo opportunity had got away. I laid down on the grass to observe it, and, much to my surprise, I watched it walk along the beach back towards the Point. It climbed onto the rocks again and made its way back towards the exact spot I had originally flushed it from! I crawled to the edge of the grass, overlooking the rocks where I had previously disturbed it, and laid down and waited, camera poised in anticipation. Sure enough, the whimbrel soon walked into view and I got my closest and best ever views of this wonderful wader as it used its long bill to look for rock creatures to feast on, pushing it deep into all the holes and crevices. No place to hide when a whimbrel is about.

This was one of the best photos that I took of it. I never dreamt I'd ever be so close to a whimbrel!

Getting close to birds without the use of a hide is very difficult. I've used general public hides on occasion of course, mainly at my local RSPB reserves, but for the most part I get bored too quickly. I like to be on the move. I'm always being told by people that I must have great patience to get the photos that I do, but actually, nothing could be further from the truth! Time is also an issue, or rather, lack of it is.

Another misconception that people have of me is that I must always be out in nature with my camera. Again, this isn't true sadly. I would dearly love to have nothing else to do but enjoy nature and capture it with my lens, but the truth is that a full time stressful job, and a young family, keep me more than occupied for the majority of my time.

When I do get the chance to take a photo or two, I have to grab it and make the most of it! Hence why I consider sitting in a hide, hoping for something to show, not the best use of my limited 'nature time'.

I managed this photo whilst out in the open, unhidden, at the Huntspill Seawall near Burnham-on-Sea. I managed to get close to a couple of ringed plovers without the use of a hide by using fieldcraft. I lay down flat on the concrete seawall and literally dragged myself towards the birds, using just my elbows and toes, and holding my camera and lens in both hands. It was agony, and painstakingly slow! Every few metres, I stopped and took a few photos. Staying so low meant I didn't break the skyline, and although the plovers were aware of my presence, they didn't ever feel threatened.

This was one of the last photos I took before I decided to back off in the same way as I had approached. The bird never moved. I hurt all over, my elbows were grazed and my t-shirt torn, but it was all worth it!

Dartford Warbler

During the spring of 2016, Dartford warblers were seen in the sea buckthorn, along the beach at Sand Bay, near Weston Super Mare. I decided that I had to visit and try and see and photograph these delightful little birds for the first time. I messaged a fellow nature photographer, Penny Wills, and asked her about the bird's whereabouts, as she had seen them a couple of days previously. When I got to the beach, the sun was out, but it was very blustery, so I wasn't holding out much hope as Dartfords do not like to sit out in the open in windy weather, and I didn't even know if they were still about.

It's quite unusual for these tiny rare birds to be so close to the coast, they're more often found on the Dorset heathlands, with a few found on the gorse and heather covered uplands of Exmoor and the Mendip Hills. They are very susceptible to cold winters, so being by the coast actually makes sense, and it is slightly warmer at this time of year than their usual haunts, though you wouldn't believe it with the biting sea winds!

I am pleased to say, I did manage to find them. Photographing them though was still far from easy! I handhold my heavy lens, and the wind was blowing me about as I tried to pinpoint my focus on these tiny birds in the undergrowth. I know it's hard to believe how much I was being buffeted about when looking at this seemingly calm photo, but I worked hard for it, believe me!

There were at least three of the warblers present, that I heard and saw, but I suspect there were a few more hidden away. This was one of my most pleasing birding encounters, I'd wanted to see and photograph these charismatic little warblers for as long as I'd owned a camera.

Wigeon and Teal

One crisp and cold morning deep in the Somerset winter, I visited RSPB Greylake's main hide, making my way along the track, noticing a few moorhens dotted about, but alas, no water rails in their usual haunt. It didn't help that all the open areas of water I'd walked past were completely frozen.

As always, there were hundreds of wigeon and teal in front of the hide, but, rather disappointingly, they were not as close as normal, as the big freeze had also claimed the water immediately in front of the hide, with only the middle of the lake left unfrozen.

Now, whilst it was rather bright, that didn't equate to it also being mild. Oh no, far from it. As soon as I lifted one of the windows to point my lens out of it, an arctic blast of freezing air hit me full in the face, causing my eyes to water and my ears to shrink. This was all I deserved. I get caught out every single time I enter this hide. I walk in brazenly, t-shirt and thin jumper, no hat, no gloves, no hot water bottle, 'It's not that cold' I say to myself as I walk past several other birders in the hide, peering at me through hats, scarves, gloves and huge, thick fleece-lined coats, shivering, teeth chattering, 'Look at that muppet; he'll catch his death in here', they probably think to themselves.

In all honesty, Greylake bird hide has to be the coldest hide in Britain. Unless there's a hide at the top of the Cairngorms that I don't know about, even Eskimos would think twice about using this hide! Frostbite is a small price to pay for the hundreds of birds outside though, and when all the ducks fly up as one, it's quite a spectacle, and allows for photos like this one. We nature photographers have to suffer for our art!

Buzzard

When I was growing up in Kent, I never saw buzzards. They were very rare in the South East of Britain. Like all birds of prey, they have often suffered persecution, particularly from game keepers. They were also affected by myxomatosis, which killed so many of one of their favoured sources of food, the wild rabbit, and in the 1960s, certain widespread pesticides reduced their ability to breed.

With so many obstacles put in their way over the years, all by humans, in one way or another, their current widespread status is both remarkable and very welcome. The 'mewing' of buzzards overhead is now a common sound here in Somerset. There have been occasions when I have driven past an agricultural field and seen over 30 buzzards loafing about in it! For such a fearsome looking bird, they do enjoy feeding on worms and other small creatures, hence why a freshly ploughed field is attractive to them.

However, whilst they may now be considered common birds, they are by no means easy to photograph. Buzzards often sit out in the open on posts and telegraph poles, close to the road, and they are perfectly happy to watch the traffic pass them by, however, if you slow down to stop and try and get a photo, they'll normally have taken flight before you even have the window open! I know, because I've tried it millions of times. You'd think I'd learn my lesson, but there's always the chance that one will go against type, and just sit and pose for a change.

The buzzard in this photo had indeed been perched on a post, but it was by the reeds at RSPB Ham Wall, not by a road. As I peered around a short line of low trees, the bird clocked me and flew off. For once I had a flight shot of a buzzard that was not a distant dot, high in the sky! It was taken during a meeting I'd organised for the 'Somerset Nature Photography' Facebook group members. I think everyone attending had a great time, although I'm quite uncomfortable around a large group of people, all due to an anxiety in social situations that I've suffered from since I was a child.

Little Owl

Guess what the smallest owl in Britain is?

Yep, it's the appropriately named little owl, a bird that isn't actually a native species, but one that was introduced in the UK during the 19th Century. One introduction in 1889, by landowner Lord Lilford, was so successful that the bird was known in England as Lilford's owl for a while.

The little owl quickly colonised much of England and Wales, helped by the fact it didn't have much competition, being a small bird of prey that favoured an insect diet. In the last 20 years though, they have been suffering a decline.

My first ever little owl was seen when I was a teenager, shortly after moving to Somerset with my family to set up a small garden centre. One morning, my dad came and got me, telling me that there was a bird caught at the bottom of one of our netted tunnels. Yep, it was a little owl! Such a stunning bird, I couldn't forget its big piercing eyes. We rescued it of course, and it flew off on rounded wings, undulating out of sight. In the years since, I've only seen them on a handful of occasions, and it's always a magical experience.

The owl in this photo was on the roof of an old barn in the village of Greinton. My timing was impeccable, as shortly after I'd visited and seen it, work began to convert the barn into a dwelling, and the bird disappeared. Something that could point partly to the reason why the little owl has declined, the gradual disappearance of old barns and ancient orchards in the British countryside as modern intensive farming methods have taken over. 'New' isn't always 'better'. For farmland birds, 'new' is actually a disaster.

Water Rail

The water rail is a secretive bird of marshes, reedbeds and damp lakeside vegetation, and is another bird that is far more often heard than seen. When they are heard, it's usually unmistakable, as among varied snorts is a loud, piglet-like squeal, quite an eerie sound the first time you hear it! RSPB Greylake is the best local spot I know to get a glimpse of these elusive waterbirds, as the damp muddy willowed area around the two main hides is very attractive to them, and in winter it's not unusual to see four or five of them feeding out in the open there.

I've managed some photos of adult water rails, from in and around the hides, but this picture is even more unusual, the one and only time I'd seen a baby water rail. I was making my way back to the car park, along the main path between the reedbeds, when I noticed a tiny ball of black fluff running about on clown sized feet, right in front of me, out in the open. As I approached, it made no attempt to hide, and in fact kept scurrying about on the path and in the grassy borders to the reeds. Parent birds are brown with red beaks and black and white barring on their flanks. They also have a cocked tail that often 'flicks' like the much more familiar moorhen's does. I wondered where this little one's parents were, and whether it was ill or disorientated.

I then noticed the chick coming back in my direction, so I slowly dropped and laid on my stomach. Getting at eye level with birds can lead to very dynamic photos, but laying down can be a bit embarrassing, especially when done in a public place! Luckily there were no other people about, so I relaxed in my prostrate position, my elbows and forearms acting as a tripod, and eventually managed this photo. One of those unexpected but magical moments that being in nature often throws up!

Sparrowhawk

It isn't only planned field trips or chance encounters whilst out exploring the countryside that lead to magical birding memories. One autumn, a brief moment viewed from my kitchen window had me excitedly running for my camera. A male sparrowhawk had come to visit my humble little garden.

Sparrowhawks have long been one of my favourite birds. Often only viewed for a second or two as one passes swiftly on a hunt, or seen swirling on the thermals, sometimes so high up that they are little more than a dot in the sky. It's rare that you get the chance for a detailed view of these beautiful birds of prey, and even rarer the chance to photograph one reasonably close.

I was making a cup of tea when my other half, Nicola, suddenly exclaimed, 'There's a sparrowhawk in the garden!' Sure enough, just a few feet away on a branch of our flowering cherry, stood the sparrowhawk, its slate grey back to us. On the handful of other occasions one has called by it always disappears again pretty soon after, apart from the time early one morning when a larger female caught an unfortunate greenfinch and proceeded to pluck and eat it at her leisure on our back fence.

The male in this picture posed quite nicely for a couple of minutes, turning his head almost 180 degrees like the possessed child in 'The Exorcist', enabling me to get a photo of his hypnotic eyes, before he decided that he'd rested long enough and flew off suddenly. A woodpigeon, sat on a neighbouring branch, was unconcerned by its presence.

The light was poor, and I was shooting at an angle through the kitchen window, but it didn't matter. Sometimes photos don't have to be 'perfect', and this was one of those times, documenting a thrilling moment in an otherwise typical autumn day.

Wheatear

I will always remember the first time I saw a wheatear. I was a young lad on holiday in Cornwall with my family. We always used to holiday in autumn due to my father's work commitments, much to the annoyance of my sister, Michelle, who used to moan about walking on Bodmin moor in the pouring rain when her friends were enjoying summer beach holidays in the south of Spain! For me, walking on Bodmin moor in the pouring rain was just about the perfect holiday.

On rare days, the sun would come out, and we'd head to Holywell Bay near Newquay to spend a day by the beach instead, temporarily putting a semi-smile on my sister's face.

Back in those days, Holywell Bay just had a basic car park and a small beach shop, which would invariably be closed for the off-season by the time we arrived. There was a small stream that ran past the car park and snaked its way down to the sea. Beyond the stream was heathy countryside with open areas of short grass. During one September, I was scanning the car park surroundings with my binoculars when they fell upon an unusual bird stood in the middle of one of the open grassy areas, tail bobbing, holding its robin-sized body as tall and as proud as it could. A wheatear! It was one of those magical birding moments as a child, a real thrill to see a bird in the flesh that I had only ever seen in books before. This was a male, slate grey/blue back, buffy-white belly and black 'mask' around its face. What a handsome bird! After a few minutes, it turned and flew out of sight, flashing the bright unmistakable white rump.

My day had been made. I was buzzing and the wheatear became one of my favourite birds from that moment on!

Of course, digital cameras didn't exist back in those days, so this is a photo of a much more recent male wheatear, having a stretch on the clifftops of Martin's Haven in Pembrokeshire, South Wales.

Collared Dove

The collared dove is one of the world's most successful species of bird, and only reached the UK in 1955, following an impressive natural expansion of its range across Europe from its stronghold in Turkey and the Balkans. It is now a common bird in farmyards and parks, and its monotonous cooing is a familiar sound in our gardens. A big factor in their success is their ability to breed all year round, as long as the weather is mild.

There are no prizes for guessing where their name comes from! A lot of bird names are literal, relating to either their appearance, their song, their behaviour or their habitat. The collared dove's neck 'collar' make it one of those appropriately named birds, and it makes perfect sense to name birds after some of their main identifying features.

I took this photo at Yatton in North Somerset. I was working beside a derelict house with a big dead tree in its overgrown front garden. Dotted about its bare branches, like fairy lights in a Christmas tree, were up to twenty collared doves. I couldn't remember seeing so many together before. As most people know, I love photographing birds in flight so I grabbed my camera from my van and got some pics of the doves coming and going from the public path that ran alongside the garden. I was pleased with some of the mid-air shots, but I'm always on the quest for something quirky and a little bit different in my photography, so this picture of four of the birds, sat in a curved line with their heads tilted and turned the same way, caught my imagination.

In all honesty, this photo wasn't going into the book at first, but when I shared it with my Twitter followers the general consensus was that is should be included. So, always one to take advice, here it is!

Spoonbill

Somerset has become a very attractive place for long legged waterbirds that have extended their range northwards from Africa and Southern Europe into the UK. My first little egret was at the Steart peninsula back in 1991, and all the birders watching it that day were very excited, so rare and unusual this all white heron was back then. Now they're common throughout the south of England and spreading north.

The Somerset Levels host an ever growing list of previously exotic and very rare waterbirds. In recent years, many have even attempted to breed, especially at the very special RSPB reserve, Ham Wall. Along with the common little egrets and grey herons, there have been bittern, which is a particular success story, cattle egrets, great white egrets, night herons, purple herons, glossy ibis, common cranes, little bittern and spoonbill.

Coastal wetlands are best for the spoonbill, a mostly all white bird, similar in size to a grey heron. I'd seen one or two of them from time to time at Steart Marshes by the Bristol Channel, but always at a great distance. One autumn afternoon in 2018, I visited the reserve with my other half, hoping to see short eared owls. We were successful in this quest, but the light was poor and I didn't manage any decent photos of them on this occasion. Before driving home, we walked to the Quantock hide as there had been three long staying spoonbills seen from there. As soon as I got to the viewing area I was thrilled to see the three birds feeding in the shallow water, right in front of the hide! Their huge spoon-shaped bills sweeping from side to side in the water in search of food, including fish, shrimps and crustaceans.

One of my photos taken that evening is now on one of the information boards on site, after the manager of this Wildfowl and Wetlands Trust reserve contacted me after seeing the pictures on my Twitter page.

By the way, amusingly, spoonbill chicks are known as 'Teaspoons'. I kid you not!

Kingfisher

I really enjoy the challenge of trying to take good pictures of the nature I come across. Sometimes the pictures are not the greatest, but I enjoy capturing them anyway. However, the aim is to get as close to perfect as I can, knowing full well that this desire is impossible. For example, I never tire of photographing common birds as I am always trying to improve on my best shot of a particular species. One such bird is the kingfisher.

In the past, I haven't had much luck with this very popular but difficult bird to photograph. Most of the stunning kingfisher shots you will have seen on social media and in books and magazines will have been taken at specialist hides, where photographers pay a lot of money to photograph 'baited' birds, a practice thought by many to be unethical, where fish are put into a tank and lowered into a river under a perch that kingfishers are known to frequent. All underwater shots of kingfishers are baited. Sometimes the tank isn't even lowered into the river, but just above it so the camera can be set up and primed on a tripod so that the shutter can be released by remote control as soon as a kingfisher dives into the tank after the trapped fish!

Some photographers do manage to get beautiful kingfisher shots naturally, but they will have invariably put a lot of time and effort into finding a reliable spot, not to mention countless hours hidden and waiting by a favoured perch. I don't have the time to stake out kingfishers and wait for them to perform or pose to get my photos, unfortunately.

All my kingfisher shots are gained by walking about in a likely habitat, camera in hand and hoping to get lucky! A much harder challenge, and the reason I was very happy with this shot, taken at Bishop's Palace moat by Wells Cathedral. When you aren't able to get detailed close up shots, composition becomes more important, and this kingfisher sat in a late autumn tree, laden in red berries, proved quite popular. I've probably sold more canvas prints of this particular picture than any other!

During Easter 2015, my family and I had a holiday at our favourite destination, Woolacombe in North Devon. We couldn't have chosen a better time to go if we tried, the weather was glorious for the whole week.

We went to Woolacombe Sands Holiday Park, as we always have a fantastic time there. The setting is glorious, situated on the side of a beautiful wooded valley with wonderful views of the sea, beach, hillsides and Lundy Island in the distance.

We always stay at the secluded Waney Edge chalets. These are six chalets, well away from the rest of the park, but linked to it via some delightful walkways through gorgeous countryside.

Such a peaceful place, the birdsong is wonderful. All around, chiffchaffs belted out their repetitive 'chiff chaff chiff chaff' song, (was a bird ever so aptly named?!) Ravens were constantly 'cronking' overhead, along with the mewing of buzzards. In the evenings, once the sun had set beyond Lundy, tawny owls called to each other from either side of the valley.

This photo of a blackbird, seemingly singing to the setting sun, was taken by the beach car park, just after we had trudged up the sand dunes after a fun day by the sea. The bird was partially hidden in a dark bush, so impossible to photograph in detail even with the sun behind me, so I decided to climb up the steps and get on the other side of it to attempt a silhouette shot, hoping that my presence and movement wouldn't scare it off before I managed to get the shot away! I needn't have worried, so engrossed in its glorious evening song, the blackbird didn't even pause, and I got the picture I wanted. A couple of weeks later, this photo won the prestigious 'Photo of the week' award on the 'Bird Guides' website, and was eventually voted one of their best twelve photos of the year!

The beautiful waxwing is a bird that I had wanted to see since I was a child. They're a winter visitor to the UK, from Russia and Scandinavia, but the amount arriving on British shores depends on the amount of berries available to them on the continent. If they are low, they move further south and west looking for enough food to sustain them, which is a high number considering each bird can eat twice its body weight in berries every day! As a result, in some years only a handful of birds visit, spending their time in the north east of the country. This means that people in the south of England have no chance of seeing them, unless they travel long distances.

I live in the south of England! Every winter, I hope for an 'irruption' of waxwings, when up to 12,000 birds arrive on a berry hunt. On such occasions they gradually move south, stripping the rowan trees, hawthorn bushes and cotoneasters of their fruit as they go. As I live in Somerset, it's usually deep into winter by the time local sightings are reported. Every time in the past when I heard about their presence close to me, the birds had invariably disappeared by the time I'd been able to go and see them.

Then, one December morning in 2012, on my partner's birthday, there was a report on the Somerset Ornithological Society's website of waxwings visiting a berry-laden tree just a few hundred yards from my house! I could not get dressed and out of the door quick enough! This was too good an opportunity to miss, even on Nicola's big day!

As I rounded the corner on a cold frosty morning, I convinced myself that the waxwings would not be there, so much so, that even after my eyes fell upon a peach-brown crested bird, picking pink berries from the end of a branch, it took my mind a few shocked seconds to process what I saw. At last. A waxwing! This photo was taken on the same tree later on that day, when the light had improved. I felt like the luckiest person in the world.

Dunnock

This is one of my 'surprise' photos, so called because I was taken by surprise by its popularity when I shared it on social media!

I like to give my pictures wacky titles sometimes, and this shot was uploaded with the caption 'Little Eddie's new dunnock catapult performed better than he could ever have hoped.'

The vast majority of people got the joke and delighted in the picture, however one person took it literally. There followed a brief exchange of 'tweets' between myself and the aforementioned disgruntled lady that I think deserves a place in this book.

Offended lady - 'Poor little bird. dunnocks do no harm and are shy little souls. They are accentors, not sparrows. Cruel.

Me - 'You do realise it was a joke don't you? This delightful dunnock was flying to a post quite happily!'

Offended lady - 'It might not have been. There are cruel people out there who would do what you so blithely joke about!'

Me - 'Have you ever heard of Angry Birds? It's a phone app where birds are fired out of cannons. It proved so popular they made a movie out of it! I doubt my jokey caption will threaten any dunnocks!'

Offended Lady - 'That's horrendous. Poor birds. I'm revolted that you tweet such vileness, be it true or not, you evil person!'

Me - You are hilarious! You're not being serious!

Offended Lady - 'Yes I am, cruel person...'

Anyone who knows me , or who follows me on Twitter, will know just how much I despise any cruelty to animals, be it the largest African beasts or the smallest bugs going about their lives, so to be called cruel, vile and evil, on a public forum, was quite laughable. A joke is a joke. There is too much misery in the world and I try to counteract that by sharing some of the natural beauty whilst also attempting to put a smile on people's faces. Unfortunately, in 'offended ladies' case, I clearly failed.

Woodchat Shrike

It was early September 2017, when I found myself for the first time at the charming Chipping Sodbury Common, South Gloucestershire, in search of a very rare woodchat shrike. My only previous shrike was seen during a holiday in Corfu many years ago when I was just a teen, a handsome male in a lemon grove.

There were other birders about, but it wasn't as packed as I expected it to be, considering the rarity of the bird and the fact it had been plastered all over social media and birding forums after first being found a couple of days previously. The lack of crowds probably had something to do with it, being a dark, damp, early autumn day, certainly not perfect photography weather, and in this modern day and age, more and more people are not simply content to see a rare bird, they want a winning picture of it as a keepsake too!

The shrike didn't show itself at first, but I had the wonderful consolation of all the whinchats that had given me the slip my whole life turning up 'en masse' in the bushes dotted around the common! I was just as excited to see my first ever whinchats than I was to see the juvenile woodchat shrike, when it finally revealed itself at the top of one of the bushes. Despite the bad light, I managed to get this photo of it with a splash of red provided by the rosehips.

Chipping Sodbury Common was an absolute delight! I didn't move further than a hundred yards my whole time there, but saw the shrike, the countless whinchats, male redstarts, wheatears, whitethroats, skylarks, goldfinches, stonechats and wrens. There was a great bird in every bush, or so it seemed! Unfortunately, I haven't had the chance to return since, but it's certainly on my 'to do' list.

My most popular chaffinch photos are usually ones of them frozen in flight; however, there are exceptions to this rule. This shot of a male on my lawn, surrounded by a carpet of fallen pink blossom from my flowering cherry tree, being a case in point.

What makes a pleasing photograph? I've asked myself this question time and again over the years, and I still don't have a definitive answer. One person's 'Picasso' is another person's pointless scribble! It's impossible for any photo to appeal to everyone, we all have different tastes and different expectations. However, composition is generally very important, and the 'rule of thirds' is used by many photographers.

This rule isn't easy to describe, so in this instance, Google is your friend! Personally, I like my birds to be looking into the frame, not out of it. So called 'negative' space can in fact be a positive, if used in the correct manner. More than anything, I find it much easier to photograph a pleasing scene than to describe it! In this sense, I have a good 'eye', I can see straight away what will make a good photo, and then I try and predict what the birds will do to make this vision in my mind come to fruition. Of course, when it comes to photographing birds, the decision on composition happens instantaneously, as you rarely have the time to think too much about it.

This photo was predicted and planned to a certain degree. I just needed a chaffinch to play ball (not literally, although that would have made for an even better photo!) I lay on my kitchen floor and stuck my Sigma lens through the cat flap and waited. And waited. I knew the pink colours of the blossom would enhance any picture of a bird that I managed to get. I have feeders in the cherry tree so some of the sunflower hearts drop to the ground and get picked up by other birds, usually woodpigeons. Finally, a male chaffinch hopped into view, posed side-on for a couple of seconds before flying away. I got the shot I was after, and then groaned as I lifted my aching muscles up off the floor. Getting this photo was worth the pain.

This photo was taken with a lens that I only owned for about one week, before returning it and asking for my money back. It was the old Sigma 50-500mm lens, and for a lot of nature photographers on a certain budget, it was the 'go to' glass for the front of their cameras, as it offered a big zoom range and enabled an impressive reach, always handy when photographing wildlife that is difficult to get close to.

It was a huge and heavy bit of kit though, especially for someone like myself, who always handholds my camera and doesn't even own a tripod. Whilst there was nothing wrong with the lens, as this photo hopefully proves, I decided it wasn't for me.

Eventually, I purchased a new Sigma long zoom, the far superior 150-600mm Contemporary. So good is this lens, I've been using it almost exclusively for over three years, and still use it to this day! Most of the pictures in this book are taken with it.

The shoveler is another bird named after its appearance, thanks to its large shovel-like bill. It's a dabbling duck, which means it feeds on the surface of water and doesn't dive for food. Their bill is lined with comb-like 'teeth', which it uses like a sieve to skim crustaceans and plankton from the water, plus seed and small organisms from mud. They prefer marshes and lagoons as a habitat and only gather in small flocks, unlike the huge winter congregations of other duck species. At RSPB Greylake, where this male coming into land was photographed, wigeon and teal probably outnumber the shovelers 30-1. The males are a handsome mixture of greens, blues, chestnut browns, blacks and whites, whereas the females are the standard mottled brown.

Amusingly, these ducks have some alternative names in different places, such as 'poor man's mallard' and 'spoony', but they're also referred to as 'spoonbills', which considering there's already a very different water bird with that official name, is confusing to say the least!

Mute Swan

I've taken many photos of mute swans over the years, and choosing one or two of them for this book was always going to be difficult. To be honest, choosing all of the final one hundred pictures was tough enough, considering I must have taken at least 250,000 photos since obtaining my first digital camera back in 2004! I like images a little 'out of the norm', in one way or another, so I've chosen this shot of a young swan coming into land on the moat at Bishop's Palace in Wells, with autumn colours reflected in the water. Although not an obvious choice, I love this photo.

Bishop's Palace is next to the famous and beautiful Wells Cathedral, and is steeped in history itself, having been the home of the Bishops of Bath and Wells for 800 years. The swans on the moat also have a special place in the history of the place, since one of the daughters of Bishop Eden taught the swans to ring a bell for food back in the 1850s. This bell ringing became a tradition at the Palace, and still goes on today, although it's not the same swans doing the ringing! The average lifespan for a wild mute swan is 12 years, so a 170 year old one is unlikely.

Mute swans are also common out on the Somerset Levels, although they're a lot less tolerant of humans, especially if they have cygnets close by. One male at RSPB Greylake is a terror during the breeding season, and once the young arrive, will not let anybody come too close, which is a problem when his family decides to spend some time relaxing beside the main path to the hides! He hisses and approaches anyone passing aggressively, I've seen people turn back around and go somewhere else on the reserve. A very wise move, an angry Swan is not to be messed with!

In 2019, I filmed two male swans fighting ferociously at Abbottsbury Swannery in Dorset. It looked exhausting for both, these fights often lead to the death of one of the swans. Luckily, on this occasion, after ten minutes or so, a female came between them and they parted, slowly swimming away to lick their wounds, one in particular looking very bedraggled, having lost many feathers. For swans, it's either love or war, there's very little inbetween!

Pheasant

The pheasant is a familiar bird throughout Britain and many other parts of the world. It originates from Asia, but has been introduced in many places, specifically as a gamebird, in fact, it's one of the most hunted birds in the world.

The numbers involved are mind boggling, with up to 43 million pheasants released every year, and that's just in the UK! The impact this has on biodiversity is anyone's guess. Respected conservationist Mark Avery expressed his concerns in a review paper in 'British Birds'.

'If we had never seen a common pheasant in the UK, and a proposal was made to release 43 million medium-sized omnivorous birds into the countryside, would it be nodded through without murmur? I think not.' he wrote.

Personally, I am anti all kinds of hunting, but especially hunting 'for fun'. It's not the pheasant's fault that there are so many of them in our countryside. The males are handsome and very photogenic, I can't help stopping my van if I see one so I can shoot it in a much more favourable way - with my camera!

The males in this photo were on the side of a hill near Bruton in Somerset. They caught my eye as one of them seemed to be displaying to the other, instead of displaying to a female like I'd expect. It was probably a territorial display that didn't ulimately come to blows.

I love pheasants, even though one almost killed me once! I was driving back to Somerset from RSPB Arne in Dorset, when I noticed something suddenly approaching like a missile to my left, its trajectory matching mine, it happened in a split second, I had no time to react. The pheasant hit my windscreen like a bomb going off, and I was showered with glass, wrestling with the steering at 60 mph, and hardly being able to see in front of me, I somehow managed to bring my van to a safe stop in a layby, then just sat there in shock. I couldn't find the body of the pheasant, and I've kidded myself ever since that it had bounced off miraculously and flown away dizzily, nursing a bad headache.

Chough

The day I saw my first puffin was also the day I saw my first chough. I promised myself not to do the obvious joke, but I can't resist; I was well chuffed to see it! It was during my first trip to Skomer Island, my mate Justin Hawkins kindly offered to wait in the queue for the tickets whilst I went and explored the hills and clifftops of Martin's Haven. The rising sun lit up the bushes dotted about the hillside opposite the ticket office of Lockley Lodge, and I was itching to climb up there to photograph any birds that might reveal themselves in the beautiful early morning light. Indeed, there were birds everywhere on the slopes! The scratchy song of the whitethroat seemed to drift out of every other bush, skylarks and meadow pipits were singing overhead then landing out of sight.

I got some beautiful shots of stonechats, wheatears and wrens. It was so peaceful, bird song was the only sound breaking the silence. As I neared the cliffs, the ground levelled out and expansive short grass replaced the bushes. In the distance, on the cliff edge, a crow was pecking about in the grass. At least, that's what I thought it was at first. Looking through my zoom lens, my heart started racing. Red legs and down-curved red bill, this was no ordinary crow, this was a chough!

I edged closer, crouched down and took this photo. My day was made, even before seeing the Skomer puffins. After a while, it took off and disappeared over the cliff edge. I walked over to enjoy the view of Skomer Island, which was closer to the Welsh mainland than I'd imagined it to be, and there on a grassy slope below me was the Chough with its partner. Amazing.

I'd forgotten that the Pembrokeshire coast was the stronghold in the UK for these rare corvids, and I had been considering visiting Cornwall in the hope of finally seeing choughs, as they had recently returned naturally to the coast there after disappearing for 28 years. The far South Western county of England has long been associated with choughs, and back in the 1700s they were known as the 'Crow of Cornwall' in other parts of the UK.

One late December, with Christmas food causing my stomach to swell to a size that would make Santa proud, I decided to drag myself off my sofa and visit Greylake.

Despite driving for a living, my love, Nicola, didn't trust me to drive her automatic motor, so I was chaperoned to RSPB Greylake, via trips to Argos, Lidl, the garage, etc etc. My patience starting to wear thin, I urged her to drive us to Greylake quickly, before clouds caused the light to diminish to such an extent that photography proved pointless. There wasn't a cloud in the sky, but from past experience, as soon as I arrive at a nature reserve, a cloud manifests itself from nowhere and precedes to hang around for the duration of my stay, often deciding to drop rain on my equipment for good measure!

After getting stuck behind every Sunday driver, learner driver, tractor and milk float in Somerset, we finally arrived at Greylake. Incredibly, the sun was still shining. A miracle!

We didn't have much time, so immediately walked to the hide, where the usual hundreds of wigeon and teal fed or rested on the wet grassland in front of us. We scanned the birds looking for anything different or unusual. There were a few mallard and shoveler, and even a lone pintail, which was roosting right in front of the hide, but would have been easily missed in the crowds. There were also a few snipe, which were perfectly camouflaged on the wet marshy ground and only noticed when they moved.

So, in the end, nothing unusual on view during this visit, but it did the trick and snapped me out of my festive lethargy, and I got pictures of the regular birds, like this colourful wigeon in flight. Nicola drove us home again, where my sofa was calling. It had missed me, as had the Christmas chocolates..

Bittern

Parking at RSPB Ham Wall early one summer, I crossed the road and had a great couple of hours birding at neighbouring Shapwick Heath.

There were a few whitethroats dotted about, plus reed buntings and reed warblers, the latter singing from deep in the reeds and occasionally giving very brief views. On the lagoon opposite the main track were a group of black tailed godwits. Progressing to the Meare Heath hide, a great white egret flew over, followed by a grey heron and a few cormorants.

After leaving the hide, I spotted a marsh harrier flying over the reeds further up the track. I walked speedily past the trees and managed to get a few distant pics. Whilst stood there, alongside Noah's Lake, a hobby flew over. Next, I heard a calling cuckoo. One flew out of the woodland at Meare Heath and landed on a dead tree in the reed bed, then another came from the other direction and landed in the same tree. The first time I'd ever seen two cuckoos together. One seemed to be displaying to the other, before they both dropped from view. Fabulous!

Shortly after, a jay flew across Noah's Lake towards its hide. A minute later and two great spotted woodpeckers flew past, only a few feet away. I saw a willow warbler in the hedge, heard and briefly saw a Cetti's warbler, a buzzard passed overhead and another marsh harrier, carrying some prey item. Swifts were shooting back and forwards across the track, so close that I could hear the swoosh! A couple of sand martins were amongst them.

Finally, the bird I had been hoping for made an appearance, rising up from the reed bed to the right and flying to the left and out of view, a bittern! I had heard their 'booming' calls constantly, but to get such a great view of one in flight was fantastic.

As I was driving out of the Ham Wall car park, I noticed the wildlife filmmaker and TV presenter Simon King, unloading some equipment from his Land Rover. I wound down the window and told him how I loved his work. He asked me if I had got any good photos and I showed him the bittern on the back of my camera. I think he approved. Lovely man. Lovely afternoon!

In the autumn of 2015, I happened upon a female wheatear at the skate-park beside Cheddar Reservoir in Somerset. I immediately felt a similar buzz to that I felt as a child when first seeing this bird, although this time it had more to do with the fact I had a great potential photographic opportunity. Despite almost my whole life of loving these birds, I'd never actually got any decent shots of one, bar a single shot of a male at Sand Point the previous year.

This female must've sensed this, as it was very confiding and posed beautifully for me, helped by a conveniently sunny morning, giving perfect light. As a consequence I pushed the shutter speed of my Nikon D7200 up to 2500 and then 3200. I wanted to catch an action shot of it hunting insects and risked the higher ISO and possible 'noise' in order to do this. My Sigma 150-600mm lens has an aperture of f/6.3 at 600mm so needs higher ISOs when the shutter is turned up high.

I got lucky when I caught the moment the wheatear was just about to take a cranefly. I was thrilled with this shot, although I bemoaned the fact I wasn't a bit taller, as the wall was hiding her legs. Still, beggars can't be choosers. I preceded to take as many pictures of this beautiful bird as I could, and she didn't mind my presence at all, even flying to within a couple of feet of me to take a fly in the grass.

It was a wonderful half an hour, one I'll never forget. That's what nature can do, lift your spirits, enrich your life and give you lifelong memories, no matter how fleeting your experiences may be!

In turn, I know that by sharing my pictures on social media, I help bring a little bit of joy to many of my followers, especially people who are unable to get out and see the birds themselves, for one reason or another. This gives me a great warm feeling. Spreading some happiness via my photography gives it a much greater meaning.

Kingfisher

Two weeks ago at the time of writing (September 2019), I finally got a shot that I've been after for years! I'd only ever seen a kingfisher hovering once before, that was at Greylake a long time ago, and I hadn't been quick enough to get a photo then because I wasn't expecting it, and the hover was literally over in a couple of seconds, before the kingfisher was away like a giant iridescent bullet.

This photo was taken at Westhay Nature Reserve on the Somerset Levels. There is a stick in front of the North Hide there, on the edge of an open stretch of water in amongst the reedbeds. Kingfishers like to fish from prominent perches, so this stick over the water is attractive to them, and some people had been getting some lovely photos here in recent weeks.

Inside the hide, a couple of people had their cameras on tripods, the huge lenses trained on the end of the stick. A bare stick. With no kingfisher on it. Personally, I find that kind of photography boring. I have to be ready for any bird that passes, that's part of the excitement and why I always hand-hold my camera. One of the photographers said that the kingfisher had passed a couple of times in the three hours that they had been sat there, but it hadn't landed on the stick. It had hovered briefly on the other side of the hide though. I decided to go and sit at that end of the hide, away from the unproductive 'kingfisher' stick that everyone was focused on. Three more people soon entered, again concentrating on the mystical stick. Shortly, a kingfisher call was heard, and one flew towards the fabled perch. Alas for the others, it decided to swerve the stick and instead flew to my end of the hide, gained a little height and hovered for a couple of seconds, right in front of me! I was ready and waiting and got the shot.

Later, when I shared the pic on Twitter, none other than Chris Packham himself commented 'Top work.' The following week, in the same hide, another birder informed me that my name was mud after getting this photo. 'People had been waiting all day for the kingfisher' he said, 'You walk in, grab the best shot of the day, and then leave!'

Rock Pipit

Recently, I met one of my Twitter followers at a Somerset nature reserve. 'Everyone knows who this man is' he said to the fellow birder he was with as I approached, 'He takes the most incredible shots of common birds I've ever seen, they're unique, never to be taken again!'

I took his huge compliment with a slightly embarrassed 'Thank you very much' and a nervous giggle. Of course, I love getting praise, as would anybody, but I'm quite a shy person and not comfortable in social situations. At least on nature reserves I am meeting people with a similar passion as myself, so have some common ground to talk about, but I get very self conscious, very quickly, and praise isn't something I've been used to in my life. Luckily, my bird photography has led to lots of complimentary words, but most is seen in written form, in comments online for example, so a lot easier for someone like myself to take.

More than anything, I feel inferior all the time, I always have and probably always will. I'm my own harshest critic of my photography, and it doesn't matter how often my work is praised, or how many of my calendars, prints or cards I sell, I still have regular times when I doubt myself and even think I'm useless! I know this is a mental weakness. I'm quite a delicate character, and an over-sensitive one too. This is one of the reasons that I love to get away from it all with my camera, somewhere in nature, far from towns, cars, other people. I stop worrying about anything and everything and I learn to breathe and compose myself. Nature is healing.

Going back to unique shots of common birds, I was very lucky to capture this rock pipit at Charmouth in Dorset as it slid down a handrail, from the top to the bottom, like a kid enjoying the slide in a park. Whilst not exactly 'common', rock pipits can be seen around rocky coasts all over the UK and Northern Europe. They're very similar to their moorland and farmland cousin the meadow pipit, but tend to be darker birds with much darker legs. This is worth knowing for where their habitats overlap and both species can be present in the same area.

Starling

Sometimes, when I haven't much time, I like to sit in RSPB Greylake car park and take photos of the little birds that come down to the feeders. During February 2015, I bumped into fellow photographer Les Moxon there, who was doing the same thing. He had already bagged the best spot for photographing the tits and finches, but he kindly invited me to sit in the back of his car so I could shoot closer too. We had a good photographic chat between capturing the birds, including this beautifully marked starling in flight. It's crazy that some people refer to starlings as 'black' birds. They appear that way at a distance, but close up they're a multi-coloured iridescent delight!

After a while, we heard from people that were coming back from the hides that there was a raptor party going on over the reserve. Two peregrines and three marsh harriers were apparently putting on a show. I couldn't resist going to see, so thanked Les for allowing me to sit in his car, then made my way towards the main hide. Halfway down the track though, I suddenly realised I didn't have my mobile phone with me. I knew I had put it in my pocket when coming out, so thought it must've fallen out in Les's car.

I ran straight back to the car park, but Les had gone. Panic! I feel naked without my mobile. Funny how we become so attached to this reasonably new technology. I don't know how I coped when I was younger without one!

So I missed the hide and the bird of prey show and I promptly drove home, despondent. Luckily, I remembered that Les had given me his card with his website and phone number on. I called him on my landline and was very relieved to hear that he had found my phone and it was safe and well. Even luckier, I had a job that night in Taunton, his home town, so was able to pop round and be reunited with my life support (which my other half calls my phone!)

I did apologise for stumbling and accidentally stepping onto Les's cream carpet in my muddy work boots, especially to his wife, who quickly rushed in with a wet cloth to clean the mess I'd made. Clumsiness is something I've suffered with since I was a toddler, It's a miracle that I manage to capture the photos I do.

Stonechat

A few years ago, I went to Sand Point, a peninsula that stretches out into the Bristol Channel at the end of Sand Bay in Somerset, with the sole intention of finding and photographing a red backed shrike, a very rare bird that I had always wanted to see but never had. One had been sighted there for a few days previous to my visit and I was hoping I'd get lucky.

One big mistake I made was in failing to take my binoculars with me. Scanning the slopes of the Point with a camera was far from ideal.

There were many small birds in the blackthorn and hawthorn bushes, but none of them were the elusive shrike. One particular bird that got me excited more than once was the stonechat. Like the shrike, it has a habit of sitting exposed on the edge of bushes and trees. There were also robins, chiffchaffs and linnets in the bushes, but alas, no shrike! I walked right to the tip of the point and sat on the rocks at the end, looking out over the Bristol Channel to Cardiff in Wales. To the left were the islands of Flat Holm and Steep Holm. My disappointment at not finding the shrike quickly ebbed away as I relaxed for a few minutes, just enjoying the peace and tranquility. It was beautiful.

As it was a warm sunny autumn day, the Point was busy with walkers, but none ventured right to the end where I was sat as it involved some awkward rock climbing, above some worrying cliffs. As I scrambled over, bemoaning the fact I wasn't as young as I used to be, I was more worried about keeping my camera safe. Luckily, I succeeded, and I also managed not to fall to my grisly death aswell, so doubly lucky!

The stonechat pics I took that day were not the best, so, as my camera and lens have been upgraded and improved since those days, I've included this photo instead, a beautiful male stonechat, shot more recently at Martin's Haven in Pembrokeshire. On this occasion, I wasn't looking (and failing) to find a red backed shrike, but I did find my first ever chough, just minutes after taking this photo!

Meadow Pipit

As well as the famous puffins, manx shearwaters and other seabirds, there is a small bird that's very common on Skomer Island, one that is probably overlooked by most visitors in their quest to see its more celebrated feathered friends. The unassuming meadow pipit is the classic streaked 'little brown job'. As its name suggests, it's a bird of open countryside, breeding on moorland and heaths in the UK and spending autumn and winter on lowland marshes and rough grassland.

This photo was taken during my first visit, in the bracken that covers Skomer. When walking across the centre of the island, the only seabirds you see are gulls, so the small birds here offer the nature photographer alternative subjects. As well as meadow pipits, this treeless area offers habitat to wrens and linnets, and during the summer, wheatears and whitethroats too.

There's another very special bird that breeds around the centre of the island, but is a lot harder to see. My mate Justin, who had invited me to join him on my first trip to the island, is owl obsessed, and the thought of possibly seeing a short eared owl excited him more than seeing the puffins! Alas, he had no luck during the five hours that we trudged about in the baking heat. Wilting, we made our way past the farm buildings in the middle of the island, on the way back to the boat, when I saw a distinctive winged shape up ahead, 'owl' I exclaimed! I managed a quick lucky action shot of it, before it dropped down into the bracken and disappeared from view. Justin, who was walking behind me, didn't see it, but stopped close to where I had seen it and waited for as long as he could for it to show again, but it never did.

He had to console himself with the humble meadow pipit instead. In fairness, it's no short eared owl, but it is a rather pretty little bird when seen close up. Widely under-appreciated maybe, but not by me!

Snow Bunting

My first ever snow bunting was seen at the very top of Glastonbury Tor back in 2006. There were people all over this famous landmark, yet this little bird was pecking about in the short grass just a few feet away from them, totally oblivious! Snow buntings are well known for having little fear of humans, probably because they don't see people in their breeding grounds in the high Arctic, so haven't developed a natural fear of them. They will know the predators that are a danger in their icy home lands, such as Arctic foxes, but the rare times they arrive in southern UK are likely to be the first time they encounter human beings!

These birds are so suited to the harsh enviroment of the Arctic that they're only one of three species to have been recorded at the North Pole. The other two are seabirds, the fulmar and the kittiwake, so the snow bunting is the most northerly recorded passerine in the world. (Passerines are all perching birds, including songbirds.)

During the winter the birds have to move south as the conditions get too severe, even for a specialist like the snow bunting! They arrive on the coasts of Scotland and northern England, but on occasions one or two will 'overshoot' and arrive in the south of England.

The beautiful and confiding snow bunting in this photo showed up in Somerset at Steart Marshes, late in November 2017. Helpfully, it spent much of its couple of days there feeding in the main car park. When I arrived to see it on a Sunday morning, there were a small group of people gathered at the gates of the Wildfowl and Wetlands Trust's work yard, where the Bunting had decided to spend some time on the ground. I got some quite distant photos, but once the crowd had dispersed the WWT warden on site said I could go in and get a closer photo if I liked. Of course, I took him up on his offer and lay down on my stomach to get some eye level pictures of the rare beauty, including this relaxed wing stretch shot. A marvellous few minutes of quality time with a wonderful Arctic traveller.

Robin

Light is so important in photography, and I know a lot of nature photographers who won't even bother to take their cameras out on dull, overcast days. The only time I'd leave my camera behind is if there was torrential rain, as this would inevitably damage the expensive equipment!

I got caught out in 2018, when I walked to the barren and rugged St David's Head in Pembrokeshire, Wales. It was dry and clear when I left the car park of neighbouring Whitesands Beach. Adorned in just shorts and t-shirt, I hiked about a mile to the Head, seeing chough and peregrine falcons on my way. Unfortunately, I hadn't anticipated a particularly violent rainstorm! I had two cameras and zoom lenses with me, but no bag or cover to protect them from the elements.

I decided that I had to take off my shorts and t-shirt and wrap them around my cameras, in the hope that they would be enough to prevent any permanent damage to my gear. I trudged the mile back to the car in just my boxers, wishing my glasses had been fitted with mini windscreen wipers so I could see where I was going, amid the biggest downpour I've ever been caught out in. I desperately hugged the cameras to my chest, trying to keep them as dry as possible under the clothing, which was dripping wet! I got some strange looks from people in the cafe by the car park when I eventually got back to the car, all but naked and absolutely drenched. I didn't care though, because my cameras seemed to have survived the soaking wet trip!

I took this photo of a robin on a drier day, but the light was just as bad. I was parked beside Sutton Bingham Reservoir near Yeovil in Somerset. There was very little about, apart from a few mallards and gulls. I noticed a robin kept hopping underneath my van, so I laid down to try and get some photos of it. After a while it flew off across the road and disappeared the other side of a fence. I casually walked over to see if it was visible still, when I noticed a pair of little eyes peering at me from the fence. Despite the poor light, I got a robin shot that's proven quite popular. It's always wise to keep your camera with you. Unless it's raining..

Mallard

Everyone knows the mallard duck. In fact, they're so familiar, they're often ignored by birders and nature photographers for more 'interesting' subjects. Not ignored by me, however! Just recently I was in a hide at Westhay in Somerset, with a group of other photographers. We were all waiting for a kingfisher to show, but whilst the others ignored everything else that passed, I was snapping away at a female mallard that gently swam across the lagoon in front of us, an almost perfect reflection of it showing in the still, clear water. I'm sure that they must have considered me mad, but the photo proved very popular when I shared it on Twitter later, along with the hovering kingfisher that they all also missed.

That photo almost made this book, but I decided to include this picture instead. Taken at RSPB Greylake, it shows a male and female mallard coming in to land, their mid-air pose mirroring each other. Unlike the tame ducks seen at parks and urban ponds, which are fed regularly, and therefore used to humans, these are proper 'wild' mallards. You can't get close to them in the wider countryside or at nature reserves, they're far more wary of people.

Mallards are dabbling ducks, which means they feed on the surface of the water, 'upending' with their tails in the air to find food, which includes invertebrates, fish and water plants. They are capable of diving, but rarely do. Some ducks are specialist divers, including the tufted duck, another species that can be seen on town and park lakes.

Mallard ducklings are particularly cute. At least until they reach the 'ugly duckling' stage! The males play no part in raising the young, so a line of ducklings will only be seen following a female. They need to stay close too, as all kinds of wildlife will take a little duckling for lunch, from pike to herons, foxes to gulls. Although we love them tiny and cute, it's in the duckling's best interest to grow up quickly!

Blue Tit

Blue tits are a favourite bird of many people, especially those who feed the birds in their gardens. They're small, common, colourful and acrobatic, which makes them very entertaining to watch as they visit feeders for seeds, peanuts and suet, often hanging upside down as they feed. Whenever I post blue tit photos on social media, they perform better than almost any of my other bird pictures, apart from puffins and possibly robins.

This photo was particularly popular. Small birds are very tough to photograph in flight at the best of times, but to catch a dynamic mid-air pose, front on from above, is extremely difficult, so I was very pleased with this one! The perfectionist in me is still a bit critical though. For example, I'd love the background to be 'cleaner' to help the tit stand out from its surroundings more, but you can't always predict where the action will occur, you just have to shoot it when it happens! In truth, this tit was fleeing a particularly aggressive robin. In fact, this photo was taken a split second after another picture in this book. See if you can find it.

When I asked my Twitter followers what they would like me to write about in this book, quite a few of them said 'camera settings'. However, I decided against that, as a book full of camera settings does not an exciting read make! Suffice it to say, this shot required a higher than average shutter speed, a higher than average ISO, a middle of the range aperature, a slight minus exposure compensation, vibration reduction turned on, plus group focus point setting, a swift panning technique and a little dollop of luck! Thrilling information, eh..

I've also been asked many times if I do workshops of wildlife photography, but alas, I do not, due to a few factors, primarily lack of time, but also my innate shyness and sometimes crippling social anxiety! It's enough for me to know that people have been inspired by my photography to get outside in nature with their own cameras.

A familiar phrase used to denote hierarchy in business and social groups is 'pecking order'. It's probably no surprise to learn that this originates from the bird world, namely chickens. The meaning is exactly the same. Within species and between species, there's a natural hierachy. In our gardens, the popular robin is pretty high in the pecking order and regularly chases other birds away from their territory and food sources.

It's fascinating to watch different birds at a table or feeder. You can often see who is highest in the pecking order if you're observant. Pecking orders in the natural world actually help to avoid expending energy and/or injury in fights. The bird lower down in this order will invariably back down to a dominant aggressor higher up the order. This is natural self preservation and survival. Although deaths rarely occur in fights, any injury will make the birds more vulnerable to disease and predators, and less desirable to potential mates.

Although I'd watched chaffinches bicker many times, I'd never really appreciated how high up the pecking order they are amongst other common species. At least, this particular male was very dominant at RSPB Greylake, guarding the seed on 'his' post against all interlopers, apart from the bigger starlings, who were wisely allowed to help themselves unhindered.

For the most part though, he spent more time chasing other birds away than actually feeding himself, always landing back on the post, standing tall and proud, boasting about his dominance! This great tit cowered down to him, unwilling to argue that the food should be shared.

It's a bit like this in my house. I am like the male chaffinch, the strong one, the boss, and my partner and three daughters are like the other birds, lower down the pecking order. Who am I kidding. I'm actually the great tit. I do what I'm told!

Coot

Everybody has heard the expression 'As bald as a coot', but not everybody can tell a coot from the similar moorhen. They're both mostly black waterbirds, seen in parks and on reservoirs, but the coot favours open water and gathers in large flocks outside the breeding season, known as 'rafts'. Moorhens do not flock together and can be found around any natural waterside enviroments, including rivers, ponds and even damp ditches. Probably the easiest way to tell the two species apart though is to remember the 'bald as a coot' saying, as the coot has a white 'forehead', making it appear bald, whereas the moorhen has a red one.

A lot of people assume coots are waterfowl, such as ducks and geese, but along with moorhens, they're actually a member of the rail and crake family of birds. Most species in this group are skulking in their behaviour, and often hard to see. Even moorhens hide themselves away at times, but coots are very much 'out there', on view, loud and proud. If they're about, they're impossible to miss!

The coot in this photo was at Backwell Nature Reserve, a small delightful wildlife haven next to Nailsea Railway Station in North Somerset. They are hugely territorial birds during the breeding season and regularly chase each other around. This one was running across the surface of the water, a process known as 'spattering', in a quest to see off a rival. Sometimes this behaviour descends into a full on fight, which can be very aggressive. They use their huge feet to battle, almost laying on their backs, their wings flapping in the water, spray flying everywhere! Usually, one of the birds will tire and make its escape when defeated, but there are times when the brutal battles end in death, the victor climbing on top of the exhausted loser whilst pecking at it, until the beaten rival drowns. Nature can be very harsh, indeed, in Holland in 2018, there was even a record of a coot attacking and drowning a buzzard whilst protecting its chicks!

I've already included a short eared owl on a post shot in this book, but had to find a space for a photo of one in flight too. In fact, I had another two shots in my original 100 pictures, this one, and a distant picture of an owl coming in to land on a post. No matter how much I love owls, I decided that three photos of the same species may be overkill. I decided to go for this picture because it was the first shot of a 'shortie' in flight that I was truly happy with.

Again, I was at Steart Marshes on the Somerset coast, a great spot during the winter to see these owls out hunting during the day. Sometimes, there can be up to eight of them on the wing at the same time, in different parts of the reserve. It's not very often they come close enough for a detailed photo in flight though. You have to have a bit of luck with where you position yourself. Their favoured hunting areas can change from day to day, depending how successful their search for voles have been in a certain place.

When I arrived at the reserve, a couple of birders told me where they had been having good views of an owl earlier in the day.

'Great' I thought, as I took myself off to the spot that they had recommended. Stood on the public footpath, overlooking one of the fields just outside the reserve's boundary fence, I could see an owl in the distance, flying up and down in front of a gathered group of photographers! 'They must be getting great shots' I thought to myself enviously. The footpath I was on skirted around the field in a loop, finishing where the fortunate band of photographers were getting their award winning pictures. I couldn't resist, I had to get over to where the action was!

After a run that turned into a jog, then a walk, and finally a near-collapse, I reached the desired area of owl heaven. But the owl had gone.

Luckily, risking a heart attack with my mad, faltering dash proved worth it, as a few minutes later I saw the shortie approaching the other side of a low hedge, coming straight towards where I was stood. I braced myself and my camera in anticipation, and the owl rose up over the hedge, right in front of me. To say I was thrilled with the resulting photo would be an understatement!

Sometimes you go out with an idea in your mind, a desired photo that you are hoping to achieve. Sometimes you fail in this quest, but you end up taking a photo that you didn't expect instead. That was the case with this shot of a pair of mute swans at RSPB Ham Wall, sleeping on a little pond beside the main car park. It was getting pretty dark, and I was on my way back to my car after going to see the huge starling murmuration that the reserve is most famous for. The sun had disappeared by the time the starlings arrived en masse, and they quickly dropped and settled into the reeds, so didn't put on a show for the watching crowds on this occasion, unfortunately.

Making my way back to the car park, I happened upon the sleeping swans. Everyone else was walking past, barely casting them a fleeting glance, but I was immediately struck by the serene scene, the contrast between the white swans and the black water and background, draped in shadows from the vegetation growing around the pond's perimeter. The fading light was far from ideal for photography, but I just had to capture the beauty I was seeing in front of me, and hope for the best with the results.

On seeing the photo on my computer screen, my partner Nicola proclaimed it one of the best pictures I'd ever taken! High praise indeed, although I didn't agree at all. Not that I don't love the photo, because I do, but because, as a photographer, I didn't have to work hard to get it! I get far more satisfaction from photos that not everyone can take. Small birds in flight for example. Anybody could have taken this photo. Having said that, countless people with cameras walked past the sleepy duo, not noticing the photo opportunity. I, however, 'saw' the shot, and I got it.

Later, this photo was framed and put up on the walls of Clavelshay Barn restaurant near North Petherton in Somerset. By all accounts, it was admired by the staff and diners alike. Just not quite as much as it was admired by my better half!

Mandarin Duck

Surely the most colourful duck in the world, the male mandarin looks like it was created in a primary school classroom by over enthusiastic youngsters with access to every paint pot available. It's a duck that originates from China and Japan, but escapes from wildfowl collections has led to them living 'wild' in small numbers around the UK. Once seen, it can't be forgotten!

Mandarins nest in holes quite high up in trees, so have not competed with other wildfowl for breeding sites. This has meant that they have not had a negative impact on our native ducks. They do have to compete with other hole nesting birds though, such as widespread jackdaws, so lack of nest sites has probably prevented the population increasing further.

The story around the male mandarin in this photo is a curious one. For a couple of years a female mandarin made her home at Cheddar Reservoir in Somerset, not far from the famous gorge. She associated with the resident mallards, and followed them around, probably for safety in numbers. Then, eventually, she was joined by a male! It was a romantic avian scene, seeing them together on the water, never leaving each other's side. It was a heart warming story. Until one day, when I visited in early 2019, and found the male on his own, the female nowhere to be seen! I hoped that wherever she had gone, she'd soon be back to her mate. It never happened though, sadly.

I took this photo as he was having a good preen of his beautiful feathers. His splayed tail, together with the combination of colours, with orange 'sails' evident, and turned head, eyes half closed as if snoozing, all contributed to a pleasing overall picture. My Twitter followers agreed, and the photo became so popular that I decided to put it on the front cover of my 2020 bird calendars, which had sold over 250 copies at the time of writing (early October 2019).

Greater Spotted Woodpecker

From the days of Woody Woodpecker, the cartoon character I loved as a kid, I've had an affinity for these special birds. I'll always remember seeing my first ever great spotted woodpecker. I was about 10 years old and living at Stace Cottages in Paddock Wood, Kent. These were four adjoining homes surrounded by orchards and countryside. The back gardens were huge, mostly lawn and vegetable plots, but close to the houses, next to our shed, stood a large tree, one that I occassionally climbed when I wasn't kicking a ball about with neighbour Daniel or listening to Shakin' Stevens with his cute sister, Jennifer Leon.

One morning I glanced out of my bedroom window and saw a black and white bird inching up the trunk of this tree, in short, jerky movements. I was absolutely thrilled! The woodpecker quickly flew off, but the moment was imprinted in my mind forever!

Now, whenever I see a great spotted woodpecker, I think about my youth at Stace Cottages. These were some of the happiest years of my life. No responsibilities, apart from getting my homework back on time, a huge garden to explore, and great friends in Jenny and Daniel. My sister Michelle and I came up with great games for us all to play. One of my favourites was sitting on our swing and seeing who could kick their flip-flops the furthest! Simple times, before mobile phones and computers, but so much more memorable and healthy. I was never bored, we made our own entertainment in those days. Even the TV had only three channels to choose from!

We were also only a short walk away from my grandad's farm, where we had lived previously. I used to regularly visit and take my binoculars to an area called 'Ten Acres', where grandad had seen a hole in one of his fruit trees where a great spotted woodpecker was nesting. I settled down at a safe distance and quietly watched its comings and goings in awe.

This photo was taken far more recently, through my Somerset kitchen window, during the extreme weather event that was the 'Beast from the East'. None of the magic has disappeared, woodpeckers still excite me to this day. Maybe it's their jerky, robotic movement, maybe it's their shyness, which means that they're not easy to observe, or maybe it's just because they remind me of a joyful and carefree time of my life

Everyone loves puffins. Whenever I share photos of them, they're always well received, even when I don't give the puffins names! They're also a bird that are photographed very often, so getting something a little different from the norm is very difficult. Often you need a bit of luck.

That's exactly what I got when I was photographing this puffin on Skomer Island. Of the many puffins dotted around me, it was this one that was buzzed by a bee, just as I was clicking the shutter button. I fired off a burst of photos when I saw the bee, and when I checked the camera screen afterwards I grinned from ear to ear. I simply could not have captured the moment any better! The puffin and the bee are eye to eye, like they're sizing each other up for battle!

The photo was taken on my second trip to Skomer. This time I took my better half, Nicola, with me. We had to hire a car for the trip as our Mondeo had developed a fault where it would literally die whenever the turbo kicked in. A very scary and dangerous fault, especially when driving on a motorway! We had gone on holiday to Pembrokeshire a few months previously and it was whilst driving up a hill on our way that the car first suddenly broke down and rolled to a halt, on a dual carriageway! Nicola was driving, our three daughters were in the back and I panicked and leapt out of the car, waving my arms at the approaching traffic to warn them about the hazard ahead. Luckily, the car started again almost straight away, and I jumped back in, my heart racing from the adrenaline. I was on edge for the rest of the journey, worried that the Mondeo could give up the ghost again at any time!

The car Nicola and I hired for our Skomer trip had no such faults, but it was pretty gutless, slowing down whenever we tried to climb a hill. Importantly though, it didn't stop completely! We stayed overnight at the delightful Foxdale Guesthouse in Marloes, and arrived quite late at 10.15pm. The owner kindly waited up for us, answering the door in her dressing gown, and when we informed her that we would miss breakfast the next day, as we had to leave early to queue for the Skomer crossing, she immediately made us sandwiches to take with us, and put them in the fridge for us to collect in the morning when we let ourselves out. What a lovely lady!

Redwing

The name 'redwing' is invariably linked with the name 'fieldfare', as they're both winter visiting thrushes to the UK, and often flock and feed together. Redwings are shy but beautiful birds, with spotty chests like their relative, the song thrush, but also sporting a clear stripe above the eye, known as a supercillium. As their name suggests, they also have a colourful splash of red under their wings and on their flanks, making them easy to differentiate from other thrushes.

I took this photo in mid-November 2018. I was on the way to hand deliver a couple of my 2019 calendars to a lady in the village of Chilton Trinity in Somerset. I drove down some lovely country lanes, and passed an area of roadside hedges draped in red berries. There were birds all over them, mainly fieldfares and redwings, but also blackbirds and robins, all of them enjoying the berry feast. I stopped my van, grabbed my camera and slowly got out. The birds hid deep in the hedge for a few minutes, but I stayed very still, leant against the van roof, and once the birds realised I wasn't a threat, they resumed feeding, coming out to the end of the branches, where the juiciest berries hung.

Most of the birds were still partly obscured by twigs, but this one fed in full view. Once it pulled a berry off, it would toss it up and catch it again in its beak. I assume birds do this because they're easier to swallow in a certain position, like kingfishers swallowing fish head-first.

The light was quite poor, as it was a cloudy day, so I had to push the ISO up on my camera as I wanted to catch the berry in the air, and such a brief, fleeting moment needed a fast shutter speed. Photography is all about compromise when it comes to your manual settings. Every setting affects another one. A fast shutter speed in poor light will lead to a dark or even a pitch black, photo! So you have to increase the light sensitivity, which then increases the chance of 'noise', a very undesired effect that leaves the photos with a grainly or blotchy appearance. So it's a delicate balancing act, but I managed the shot I wanted, thankfully without too much of the aforementioned noise!

Pied Wagtail

My first memory of these charming little birds was as a child on my grandad's farm in Kent. I used to see them regularly running across the farmyard in pursuit of flies and bugs, their long tails bobbing constantly. The poet John Clare described them delightfully 'Little trotty wagtail he went in the rain, And tittering, tottering sideways he ne'er got straight again'.

My grandad always called them 'Peggy Dishwashers'. There's a whole range of old country names for them, probably more than any other bird!

They're usually seen in ones or twos, but on cold winter nights they will flock together to roost, often in town centres or supermarket car parks, where it is slightly warmer than the exposed wider countryside. I saw this for myself when I was travelling down to Kent with my other half a few years ago. We stopped at a supermarket in Wincanton to stock up on supplies as darkness started to fall. Getting out of the car, I could hear numerous pied wagtail calls, and noticed a few of the birds on the ground. After coming out of the supermarket a few minutes later, the wagtail numbers had increased at least tenfold, and more and more were descending out of the dark sky, to be lit by the car park lights.

We watched the spectacle for a little while, many of the birds settling into the trees dotted around our car. There must have been hundreds of birds! Eventually we had to get on our way, as we had a long journey ahead of us, but were thrilled to witness this unexpected natural delight.

I took this photo at Kilve Beach in Somerset, where Bryan Adams had made the video for his mega hit '(Everything I do) I do it for you.' Pied wagtails are insectivorous, so are expert bug hunters. As my partner and three daughters looked for fossils, I sat down on the rocks trying to photograph the wagtails as they hunted. Timing the exact moment they take off after a passing fly is extremely tough, so I was delighted with this picture, one that quite nicely sums up much of the life of the Peggy Dishwasher!

There are few birds that are as intrinsically linked to the start of spring as the swallow. To many people, spring doesn't begin until their first sighting of one of these much loved visitors from South of the Sahara Desert in Africa. They are often confused with the similar looking swift, but they are not even distant relatives. Instead, swallows are members of the hirundine family of birds, which include another regular summer visitor, the house martin.

Swallows are very fast fliers, and their flight pattern is unpredictable, often twisting left or right, or suddenly changing direction altogether! This makes them one of the most frustrating and challenging birds to photograph in flight. I can't be the only one who regularly tries, and fails, to capture swallows in mid-air! I've had some half-decent efforts in the past, but nothing as good as this picture, taken at Martin's Haven in 2019, shortly after disembarking the ferry from Skomer Island. In fact, in my eyes, this photo was better than any of the puffin pictures I had caught earlier, purely because of the difficulty factor involved!

Totally unconnected to this specific pic, one of my social media followers, Jenna Myles, had been admiring my 'bird in flight' photos for some time, and in 2019 she invited me to be a special guest on her community radio show, 'Somerset Cool', on FromeFM, to talk about birds and my photography. For a whole hour, totally live! I was very flattered to be asked, but also very nervous. When I arrived at the studios, she immediately put me at ease with her bubbly and friendly personality, and the hour on air flew by! In fact, it went so well, she later invited me on again, to take part in her marathon 24 hour live show, raising money for causes close to her heart. It was an honour to do so.

You can imagine how thrilled I was, when in November 2019, Jenna beat all challengers to win the 'Best Newcomer' award at the 'National Community Radio Awards'. No-one deserved it more.

When it comes to cute birds, they don't come much cuter than the long tailed tit. Seldom seen on their own, they often roam the countryside in loose flocks, looking for food, sometimes with other tit species, goldcrests and chiffchaffs. They constantly call as they move through trees and bushes, and their high-pitched 'si si si si's' are often the first indicator of their presence. Flocks are usually family groups, and this calling is so that they all keep in contact on their way. If you're lucky, they'll come to the end branches on the outside of the bushes and give you a good view. More often than not though, they frustratingly look for bugs and spiders deep inside the bushes, and are only seen clearly as they set off on the usually short flight to the next tree, their disproportionately long tails following faithfully behind them.

Winter is an arduous time for most birds, but particularly for the long tailed tit. It's harder to find their favoured invertebrate food, so the flocks will come to gardens and take seeds, nuts and suet to help them get through the harsh cold months. They are tiny birds, so need to eat regularly to maintain their health and improve their chances of surviving a freezing night. Another survival tactic is to cuddle up close as they roost, sharing their body heat. If it wasn't for their long tails, they'd be the smallest bird in Europe, even smaller and lighter than goldcrests and wrens!

Long tailed tits are many people's favourite bird, including my partner Nicola. I'm a big fan myself, although my favourites change like the British weather. I love all birds!

This photo was taken at RSPB Swell Wood near Fivehead in Somerset. It's the site of one of the biggest heronries in the West Country, but also a great place to see the common woodland birds. The birds are fed in the car park, and I have access to the locked bins where the seed is housed. When I am passing I will fill the feeders if they need it. Birds will come down immediately, including nuthatches and various tits. This long tailed tit miraculously stayed still long enough to let me take its picture.

Carrion Crow

Within an hour of getting the Sigma 150-600mm Contemporary Lens, I captured this image of a juvenile carrion crow begging its approaching parent for food. Although I was happy with this shot; which was taken near my Somerset home back in 2015, I did have some concerns about the lens itself. Here's what I wrote on my blog after that first trip out with it.

'If I'm honest, after using the lens in bright conditions for a day, I was a little disappointed with the sharpness. I've always used a Nikon 70-300mm VR lens, quite a cheap lens, but surprisingly sharp. Being much smaller and lighter than the Sigma, though, makes it easy to handhold steady. The 600mm, by comparison, is a beast. Even with good technique, when you look through the viewfinder the subject is jumping all over the place! The lenses optical stabilisation does a good job. The other option of course is investing in a tripod. However, I find them too restricting, I like the instant capabilities of hand holding, as with nature, things happen quickly and you need to be ready to capture it. I would miss most of my shots with my camera on a tripod!

It might just be a case of getting used to the lens and accepting the trade-off of twice as much 'reach' but less sharp pictures. This is the conundrum all nature photographers on a budget face, we all want sharp pictures with a decent reach, but can't afford or justify spending £6000 or more on 600mm Nikon prime lenses!'

Over four years later, I now love this lens! Most of the images you see in this book are taken with it. It's not perfect by any means, but it's a versatile and affordable nature lens and I would recommend it to anyone wanting to take up the challenging, but very rewarding world of bird photography. The ability to zoom in and out of a shot isn't possible with the sharper prime lenses, but for me, it's extremely important to have this zooming capability.

Song Thrush

When I was a lad living in Kent, the song thrush was as common in our garden as the blackbirds were. Both species loved our lawn and were expert worm catchers. The song thrushes also left snail shells dotted around, where they had smashed them against stones or other hard surfaces, known as anvils, to get at the soft tasty creatures inside. No other bird does this.

Fast forward to the present day, and the decline of the song thrush is truly shocking. Out and about on the Somerset Levels, I see kingfishers far more often than I do these thrushes. In fact, in the whole of 2019 so far (it's mid-October as I write), I can only recall seeing or hearing them a maximum of four times!

As a result, song thrushes are on the Red list of UK birds, which means they're of the highest conservation priority, needing urgent action. So scarce are they, that when one visited my garden earlier in the year, I immediately tweeted the exciting news to my followers. It had been ten years since I'd seen one from my kitchen window!

I took this photo at Apex Park in Burnham on Sea. I love bird pictures with surrounding splashes of colour, so red berries are perfect. As its name suggests, the thrush had been singing beautifully. It's one of my favourite bird songs. Years ago there would be one singing every evening in the trees behind my garden. I'd sit on my swingseat silently and listen to the gorgeous melody, echoing across the neighbourhood. I'll never forget the sense of peace and calm that came over me during those magical evenings, and I really hope to experience them again.

Poets have long been inspired by their glorious song, with the nineteenth century British poet Robert Browning writing;

'That's the wise thrush; he sings each song twice over,

Lest you should think he never could recapture,

The first fine careless rapture'.

Woodpigeon

Woodpigeons are quite comical characters. Watching them bicker and size each other up in dispute over a mate is rather amusing to watch, even though to them, it's a serious business. They are now a common bird in UK gardens, but it wasn't always the case. Growing up, they were a rather shy bird of farmland and countryside. Their gradual move into gardens coincided with the increased popularity of feeding birds. Coming into more human contact has consequently stripped them of much of their shyness, and I can now sit quietly in the garden and watch them come down to have a drink from the bird bath, literally two metres away.

Once they have found a mate, they can be very tactile and loving birds, as this photo, taken at Backwell Lake, demonstrates. They sit side by side, cuddled up close, and preen each other's feathers. This strengthens their bond. A few years previously, I'd taken a very similar photo at the same location. It proved to be extremely popular at the time, but looking back, the quality wasn't great, as it had been taken with an older camera and lens and had to be cropped a bit too much. I was closer to this pair, and I also had a zoom lens with twice as much reach, so I could watch and photograph without disturbing them. Not that they were paying much attention to the world around them!

As with most birds, woodpigeons have a crop, a muscular pouch where food collects after eating, waiting to be digested. The crop of the woodpigeon can hold up to 1000 grains of wheat! Crops enable birds to feed quickly, taking in much more food than they could possibly digest straight away. This is important, as sometimes food can be scarce and it enables the birds to store food to digest at a later time, it's also safer, as birds tend to be more vulnerable to predation when they are feeding. Woodpigeons digest their food during the night as they roost. They also produce 'crop milk' to feed their young. This isn't a dairy product though, but partially digested food. Yum.

Great Crested Grebe

There are very few waterbirds as graceful as the great crested grebe. Their courtship dances are one of the natural world's most beautiful displays. However, I've never had much luck seeing them, unfortunately. I can only remember twice witnessing the magical moment when a pair swim towards each other, carrying a gift of weed in their beaks, and rise up out of the water, belly to belly, heads flicking left and right, feet paddling like mad! Both of these occasions were at Chew Valley Lake near Bristol. The first was almost 20 years ago. My other half Nicola was heavily pregnant with our first daughter, Emily Jane. She wasn't best pleased that I had dragged her through wet, boggy woodland to reach a remote hide by the lake! It was whilst there that we watched the magical mating dance of the grebes. Unfortunately digital cameras didn't exist back then, so no photos were taken, but the images live on in my mind.

It was during the walk back to our car that I started to worry about Nicola suddenly going into labour! There were no other people around, just trees and wet muddy pathways, which probably would be more of a hindrance than a help when delivering a baby! Luckily, Emily Jane stayed put, and we made it back to the car safely, albeit with very damp feet! I was also rewarded with great views of my first ever redpoll. Nicola ached all over, and was relieved to rest her legs once we reached the car. In fact, she almost used those very same words. 'Hey Carl, I'm relieved to rest my legs now!', she said, or words to that effect, give or take a few choice expletives.

Emily Jane arrived about a week later. There was a bit of drama when the umbilical chord got wrapped around her neck during birth, and she was whisked away by the doctors, but she was soon returned, thankfully, safe and well.

I took this photo in the spring of 2019 at Apex Park in Burnham-on-Sea. I had hoped to photograph the mating dance, and was laying on my stomach at the lake edge. Again, I had no luck with that, but this grebe popped up right in front of me after a dive, and allowed me the consolation of a close portrait shot.

Raven

Ravens are wonderful corvids. They're much larger than the other crow species, and can be recognised in flight by their wedge-shaped tail and deep 'cronking' call. They're much shyer than rooks and crows, so I was delighted to get this photo at West Bay in Dorset, the coastal village where the ITV drama series 'Broadchurch' was filmed.

There was one time when I hoped to photograph a raven that I wasn't so lucky. In fact, I could have died!

I was working on the main road near the top of Pen hill in Somerset, part of the Mendip range. I'd been noticing buzzards and ravens overhead, so when my lunch break arrived I grabbed my camera and made my way across the open hilltop towards the Mendip TV Mast, the tallest structure in South West England. Keeping my eye on the sky, I suddenly noticed movement on the brow of the hill. To my horror, a herd of cows appeared, and started running at speed, straight towards me! Feeling extremely vulnerable, and too far away from the safety of the road, I had no choice but to run in panic towards a small copse of bare trees further up the hill, praying that I didn't trip and get trampled by the marauding Friesians!

I made it to the copse in time, just, and launched myself up the nearest tree, with squirrel-like athleticism, only to find that it was a dead tree, its skeletal branches snapping as soon as I grabbed them, depositing me unceremoniously back on the ground! The Herd of Terror were almost upon me, and I managed to pull myself up a neighbouring tree, my camera and lens flapping about wildly, hanging from my neck.

The cows gathered around and stared up at me, as if they'd never seen a human being before. I tried 'shooing' them away, it didn't work. I tried shouting, it didn't work. I thought I was going to be up in the dead tree all night, but after about 20 minutes, which felt like forever, they grew bored and started to filter away. Once they were all out of sight, I gingerly climbed down and nervously crept out of the safety of the copse, before sprinting across the open ground towards the main road, once I saw that the coast was clear. I never did get the raven, but I left that place with my life..

Reed Bunting

I'll always remember seeing my first ever reed bunting, I was only a young boy and I saw it in my Kent garden. There were no reeds nearby, indeed, there wasn't even a river close to us, or any open body of water! However, there was thick snow on the ground and it had ventured into our garden to eat the seed my mum had put out for the birds. During freezing weather, all kinds of birds will visit gardens looking for food and water. One year, a moorhen turned up in my little Somerset garden during a snowstorm, it was surreal watching it running around pecking up seed, then hiding under one of our bushes, seemingly unsure of this alien environment.

Nowadays, reed buntings will regularly come into gardens during the winter looking for food, it doesn't even have to be freezing. It's a learned behaviour that has helped them survive harsh conditions in their usual habitats. Feeding birds is rewarding for us, but it's absolutely essential to many of our feathered friends. It can cost quite a bit, but is worth every penny. Putting water out is also just as important, especially when everywhere is frozen. All the food in the world will not keep a bird alive if it can't drink regularly! A plant pot base is perfect, just top it up regularly, keep it clean and make sure it doesn't freeze. Lots of birds will bathe in the water too, which is always entertaining to watch. They genuinely look like they're having fun as they splash about, but it's very important to keep their feathers in good condition.

This photo of a female reed bunting taking off was taken at RSPB Greylake, the best place I know to see them up close. They regularly come to the car park feeders and have grown quite confiding, showing little fear of people, as long as you sit or stand quietly and don't make any sudden movements. I'd never have thought, all those years ago when I was an excited lad seeing my first ever reed bunting, that I would ever be able to watch them close up, whenever I wanted, where they were just as common as blue and great tits!

Goldfinch

Goldfinches love teasel, but it's not often you see them in such good light with a nice background and very little in the way of distractions, as in this picture. I was at Steart Marshes in Somerset, looking for short eared owls, when I saw this pair looking for seeds in the teasel heads. I remember seeing a couple of people on a footpath just behind them, getting closer with every step, and I had to take advantage of the opportunity to get a decent photo before the birds were inevitably scared away.

Frustratingly, their red faces were turned away from me (the goldfinches' faces, not the people's), and I quickly got closer, staying low and steady. When a safe distance away, I went down on one knee, not to propose to the birds, but to use my other knee to rest my elbow on so I became a slightly less stable human tripod. Just at the right moment, one finch flew, and the other helpfully lifted its head up, and I was primed and ready to grab the shot. Luckily, they were about the same distance from my lens, so both birds were sharp.

This picture pretty well sums up my whole bird photography philosophy. A lot of nature photographers go out with a specific idea or species in mind, and an image in their head that they are after, often putting many hours or days into that quest, staking out favoured spots, observing the behaviour of their chosen subjects, setting up hides or donning complete camouflage, from head to toe, so that they blend into their natural surroundings. Then they wait, and wait.

I don't have the time or patience for this. I sometimes go out hoping to photograph a certain species, such as the owls I was looking for on this occasion at Steart, but my best photo of the day was of these common goldfinches, which I just happened upon whilst walking about, enjoying the countryside and fresh air. I find this very rewarding, and it's how I love to do things.

One of my favourite spots for taking pictures of birds is at the Lake Grounds by the beach at Portishead. I found this place by accident in 2011 whilst working nearby, and have returned a number of times when in the area. There are a variety of habitats within a small area, with the lake itself, the surrounding lawns and park, and just across the quiet access road is the beach, with saltmarsh, rocks, pebbles and mud, which waders love. A short walk takes you up to Battery Point, with views across the Bristol Channel to Wales. The thick bushes here give shelter to a variety of little birds and the short grass is popular with blackbirds.

Whenever I visit, there are a number of birds I always see, without fail, including rock pipits, linnets and pied wagtails. I don't always manage good photos of them all, but I got lucky with this wagtail. It was hunting bugs on the grass between the road and the lake. I had been trying to get it in flight as it chased a fly, a very challenging type of photo. As I was looking through the camera I could see it trying to eat something tiny, and, as I was a fair distance away, I thought it had succeeded, as they usually invariably do. Not much will escape a wagtail on the hunt!

It was only after I had got home and uploaded the photos to my computer that I noticed the weevil clinging onto the top of the wagtail's beak for dear life! Even more incredibly, as I had taken a series of pictures, I could see that the weevil started off inside the beak and had managed to shift itself around to the relative safety of outside of it. The bird seemed oblivious, the weevil was hidden in plain sight, and as the sequence went on it was still clinging on as the bird wandered off into the distance and out of view. I will never know the fate of this tiny bug, but for once I'd like to think it got away with its life, it had certainly earned some good fortune!

Cute robins can actually be real terrors. It seems apt that I am writing this at Halloween, because when it comes to terrorizing other garden birds, the robin is probably only beaten by the sparrowhawk! Their endearing red breast serves a more serious role than most people realise. Males use it to settle territorial disputes with each other. The bigger and brighter the red, the stronger the robin. Usually just showing off their chests to each other is enough for the quarrel to be settled, but sometimes the robins are closely matched and a fight can ensue, which sometimes results in death.

Squabbles with garden birds of other species rarely descends into anything as serious, it seems that robins are just quite grumpy characters and sometimes won't tolerate certain other small birds on their patch! A few years ago there was a thick covering of snow in my Somerset garden, and whenever a pied wagtail landed to take advantage of the food I'd put out, a robin would fly in and chase it away. Every time!

This photo was taken at one of the bird tables at RSPB Greylake. The robin was already feeding when the great tit landed, and the resulting action all happened in a split second blur. Luckily, I got the shot! The next day I was contacted by a news agency about the picture, and the day after that it appeared in a national newspaper, the Daily Express.

I was also contacted by the Daily Mail, who wanted to do a double page spread on me and my photography, particularly the small birds in flight, after their picture editor spotted this picture on my Twitter account. Unfortunately, it coincided with the Brexit story really taking off, and they didn't have enough room for features, so it was never published. I was disappointed, but they sent me £200 anyway 'for my inconvenience'. Easy money maybe, but I'd much rather have had my work displayed in a national newspaper!

Black Headed Gull

I doubt there are many spieces of birds that I've photographed more than the black headed gull. It's a bird that just screams 'photograph me!' Any body of water is likely to have these gulls nearby, and if you take your kids to feed the ducks, expect to feed the black headed gulls too! They're loud, boisterous and impossible to miss, so they're not very popular with many people. I, however, love them. This won't be a surprise to anybody who knows me, as there isn't a bird that I don't like. They all play their part in a healthy environment, and they're all just surviving, in often very difficult circumstances.

In reality, 'brown headed gull' would be a more accurate name for them, as they're not black at all, although they appear so at a distance. After breeding, their heads turn white, with just a little brown smudge behind their eyes.

The bird in this photo had a white head. Please trust me on this..

As a general rule, if you don't capture the head, a bird photo is worthless. This is when the delete button is usually reached for. However, occasionally a picture can work really well despite breaking the accepted, yet unwritten, rules. This gull thought it was a dabbling duck, constantly upending at Sutton Bingham Reservoir near Yeovil, looking for food just below the surface of the water. I managed to catch the exact moment it upended, with the ark of water struggling to catch up with the gull. This is what made the photo something a bit different.

So here I am, scrolling through hundreds of pictures of black headed gulls for this book, and choosing the only one where you can't even see its black, white or brown head at all! Just call me a rule-breaker..

Blue Tit

I love to try and capture birds amongst blossom, but it's far from easy, and you need a bit of luck, as you do in any wildlife photography. My best chance is in my own garden, where we have an ornamental flowering cherry tree, not far from the house. Although not native, I've always loved their gorgeous pink blossom, so for a couple of weeks in spring I stand in my eldest daughter's bedroom, at eye level with the top of the tree, and hope to get a clear shot of one of the small birds coming down to my feeders.

The biggest challenge is the light, as my garden is South-facing, so on a sunny day the birds are partially silhouetted or with a harsh side light. On a grey day, it's just too dark to get decent photos. My best bet is a bright day with some light cloud cover, and mornings are better than afternoons.

This photo of a blue tit in my garden was cheekily titled 'Blue tit smelling the cherry blossom' when I posted it on my social media sites, and it was very popular. The reality though, is that the tit was looking for bugs and spiders, that hide themselves away within the pink petals. I have found that a title or a caption enables a photograph to really take off when sharing it on the internet, it compliments the picture and gives it a lease of life sometimes greater than the sum of its parts. I doubt this picture would have been so well received if I had titled it 'Blue tit looking for bugs in blossom'.

Other tits that visit gardens are long-tailed, great and coal tits, and gardens next to woodland may also have marsh tits, but the blue tit is the only one with any blue in its plumage, and is the commonest visiting tit, so shouldn't be mistaken for any of the others. It's estimated that 98% of British gardens are visited by blue tits in the winter, for food, water and shelter. So making your garden 'bird friendly' is an easy, but very important thing that you can do to help nature, and the birds will repay you tenfold in entertainment alone, not to mention the proven health benefits of watching our feathered friends!

Chaffinch

Battling male chaffinches in mid-air is a photo subject I've been after ever since I first picked up a camera. This is a rarer occurrence than battling goldfinches, who go beak to beak constantly when bickering over food, so therefore give you more opportunities to photograph them. Chaffinches don't tend to visit feeders in such tight groups, so they clash with each other far less often.

Having said that, sometimes a particularly pumped up and territorial male chaffinch will challenge any other chaffinch coming close to a food source, male or female. Indeed, as seen elsewhere in this book, they will challenge other species too!

I took this photo at my favourite local spot, RSPB Greylake. It was one of those special moments when I thought that I had finally got the shot, but wasn't certain until I scrolled the images on the back of my camera. Usually I wait until I get home to do this, but I just had to check there and then, and I let out an exclamation of triumph when I saw this pic! I quickly 'locked' the image, so I couldn't accidentally delete it. (Believe me, I'm capable!)

In the first couple of years of taking photos I was quite naive. I'd upload my pictures from my camera to my PC and that would be it, I didn't back them up anywhere else. I soon learnt a very hard lesson though. One day the electric suddenly went off as I was sat at my computer. I wasn't that bothered at first, it had happened many times before. However, when I started the PC again later in the day, I just kept getting a fatal error message and it wouldn't reboot. To cut a long story short, I found out the hard drive had been corrupted during the power outage, and it couldn't be fixed, meaning I lost every single photo I'd taken in those two years including pictures of my young daughters! I was absolutely gutted, as you can imagine. Now I copy all of my photos to an external hard drive, just in case!

Cuckoo

Few birds are as famous for their call as the cuckoo. Their name is onomatopoeic, which means it's derived from their call. It's a sure sign of spring, and an annual event for lots of nature lovers, the first time of the year that they hear a cuckoo . Unfortunately, this is becoming increasingly rare, as cuckoos have declined markedly and are now on the Red list of UK birds, meaning they're of the greatest conservation concern.

Luckily, they're still regular visitors to the Somerset Levels, particularly in and around the many nature reserves. The first time I ever saw a cuckoo was at Shapwick Heath Nature Reserve about 15 years ago. I'd heard them many times before, both in Kent, where I was brought up, and in Somerset, but frustratingly, had never seen one until that moment. The bird was in flight and went right over my head. I learnt something new that day, cuckoos also call in flight!

Of course, everyone knows that cuckoos lay their eggs in the nests of other birds, and play no part in bringing up their own young, but not many know that adult cuckoos only spend about six weeks in the UK every year! After the female has laid eggs in up to 20 different nests, adult birds return to Africa, leaving the unfortunate host birds to bring up their young. Around reedbeds, the favoured host for a cuckoo is the reed warbler, a tiny bird in comparison! It amazes me that the host will keep feeding the growing cuckoo chick, even when dwarfed by it! I'd love to photograph this incredible behaviour, but have yet to even see it.

As with kingfishers, most great cuckoo shots will have been taken from specialist hides, or will be of 'Colin', a famous, ridiculously confiding cuckoo, that has been visiting Thursley Common in Surrey for the last few years, being fed mealworms by the dozens of gathered photographers, enticing it closer.

This photo was taken at RSPB Greylake, and is a proper wild bird. I heard it 'cuckooing' first, then crept around the track by one of the small lakes until I was able to get a clear shot without disturbing it. I was thrilled!

Barn Owl

I'm often asked what is my favourite bird, and I can never give a definitive answer, as it's a bit like being asked which of my three daughters I love the most! However, if really pushed, I'd probably choose the barn owl as my favourite of the favourites.

Like many birds of countryside and farmland, they are sadly in decline. This makes seeing them even more magical, as it's quite a rare event. If I had to hazard a guess at how often I see them, I'd say no more than two times a year, and most of the time it will be a fleeting glimpse at dusk or in the blackness of night, a flash of white feathers in my headlights as I'm driving across the Somerset Levels.

A couple of years ago, during the summer, a barn owl had been reported to be coming out to hunt over the reedbeds at RSPB Ham Wall, long before it started getting dark. It was seen regularly after 8pm from the main Avalon Hide on the reserve. I'd always wanted to get a decent barn owl photo, but their scarcity, coupled with their mostly nocturnal habits, meant I hadn't had much luck on that front. So I couldn't resist visiting Ham Wall one evening after work. I made my way to the hide and walked in on a group of camera wielding owl 'hunters', all hoping to get lucky, just as I was! The evening sunlight was stunning, and after photographing cattle egrets and pochard in flight, the owl was spotted in the distance, and an electric charge of excitement coursed through the hides inhabitants!

The owl flew up and down at the back of the reedbeds, but frustratingly, stayed just out of range for the assorted cameras and long lenses pointed hopefully in its direction. Then, a bit later, it flew behind a patch of woodland to the right of the hide and made its way towards us from the back. We all filtered outside, but I missed the closest shot, as the reeds were too high, but I got this photo instead, as I shot into the setting sun. It wasn't the photo I intended, but the colours, light and atmosphere meant I left happy!

Hen Harrier

The hen harrier. What a bird! If I were Chris Packham, I'd now be rubbing my thighs in excitement at the very mention of this iconic and almost mystical bird of prey. Unfortunately, hen harriers have a long history of persecution that still goes on to this day. The main culprits are game keepers on northern grouse moors, the very same habitats that the birds call home. There's a clear and obvious conflict of interest here, but the Countryside Alliance are in denial. I had a Twitter disagreement with their Chief Executive, Tim Bonner, who claimed he loved seeing hen harriers when out on the moors and was adamant that they weren't being targeted, despite scientific research and prosecutions proving that they are. He even invited me up to the grouse moors personally to show me around, but I politely declined his offer.

This photo was taken at Steart Marshes in Somerset. During the winter, hen harriers leave the moors and move south to lower ground. This bird is a 'ringtail', a regularly used name for a female bird. Males are a stunning slate grey, but both sexes have the distinctive white rump.

I was looking for short eared owls whilst my family were looking for fossils on the neighbouring beach. Suddenly, various waders took to the sky, calling loudly. I immediately scanned the edge of the marsh for a bird of prey, and sure enough, a raptor appeared. The flash of the white rump confirmed it was a hen harrier, and I only just managed to control my excitement enough to focus on the bird as she glided past, before disappearing from view, as quickly as she had appeared!

Funnily enough, my first ever hen harrier sighting was almost at the exact same spot, 28 years previously! A beautiful male that loomed out of thick fog, crossed my path in low flight, before being swallowed up again by the gloom. A brief, but very memorable, encounter.

Coal Tit

The smallest European tit, the coal tit is a tiny bird that often comes into gardens looking for food during the winter when its natural food of insects and fir seeds are scarce. They often visit singly, grab a sunflower heart, then fly off to eat it out of sight. This means that they can easily be missed by the casual observer, who is not likely to miss the less shy and more numerous blue and great tits. As you can imagine, they're not an easy bird to photograph, especially away from feeders.

I took this photo at RSPB Swell Wood in Somerset. Woodland birds come down to the feeders dotted around the natural car park, and even then, they are extremely swift, shooting back and forth in a blur! The sheer numbers can be mesmerising, you often don't know where to point your camera!

Just down the road from Swell Wood is the village of Fivehead. It was here that I was asked to join some other local nature photographers in exhibiting our work by the Rev Laurie Burn, The Pastor of Fivehead Baptist Church, himself a passionate nature lover and photographer. It was an honour displaying my photographs alongside people like Chris Hooper and Colin Lawrence, friends that I've met over the years whilst walking the Somerset Levels with my camera.

The first ever time that I exhibited my pictures was actually the year before in Shapwick, when I was asked to join Chris, Colin and a few others in displaying our work by the Rev Richard Tweedy, the Vicar of the Polden Wheel Group and another keen bird photographer! I had a great time, and on the last evening my other half and I joined Richard and his wife and the other exhibitors at an entertaining talk by naturalist and author Dominic Couzens.

Great White Egret

I find photographing egrets a bit of a nightmare, especially on bright sunny days. They're so brilliantly white that it's difficult to set the correct camera exposure for them if the sun is glaring off their feathers, and it's so easy to 'blow out' the details, so all you have is a big ill-defined, long-necked blob. This is when it can be advantageous if the sun is behind the subject, giving the opportunity for backlit pictures.

Great white egrets are another exotic but increasing heron species to have colonised the Somerset Levels in recent years. Like the little egret, I can see them spreading far and wide, they certainly seem at home on our shores.

During a brief stop at Cheddar Reservoir, when the water was low, I saw not one, but two of these majestic birds. They were with various other herons, who were finding it easier to hunt and find their prey in the exposed mud and shallow water. Unusually, they were far away from their usual reedbed fringed wetland homes, and one in particular allowed me close enough to rattle off a few shots. The sun was behind the bird, which allowed for some pleasing backlit images, especially when it flew even closer to where I was positioned, giving me the chance to take this photo, with the sunlight coming through the wings as it landed. Again, it satisfied my desire for photos that are a bit different from the norm.

I saw this bird expertly catch three or four fish until a group of people came down to the water's edge, consequently scaring it off to the other side of the reservoir. This behaviour annoys me. They could see the bird, it was impossible to miss, they could also see me taking photos of it, yet they still walked between us and made it fly away, without a care in the world. Sure, they didn't break any laws, but as far as I'm concerned, they displayed pure ignorance. Luckily for me, I'd already got the shot I wanted!

Like many pictures in this book, this photo was taken at RSPB Greylake, which isn't surprising considering it's only about three miles from my house and is my 'go to' place if I have a spare hour or two to get my nature fix. Greylake is a fairly new reserve, having been purchased by the RSPB in 2003. Before it was managed for nature, it was arable farmland. The transformation in the ensuing years has been incredible, now the area teems with all kinds of wildlife and is so easy to get to and enjoy, laying right beside the busy A361, Taunton to Glastonbury road.

A couple of years ago, I created a Greylake Facebook Group, where members could post their sightings and photos from the reserve, and at the time of writing it has 685 members! It's become so popular that a while ago I was messaged by the RSPB asking me to put the word 'Unofficial' in the group name, so people wouldn't think it was officially endorsed by them. The success of the group led to me creating another one, the 'Somerset Nature Photography' Facebook Group, mainly because some photographers were posting pics taken at other reserves, and it was time consuming to remove them all! This new group quickly overtook the Greylake one in terms of membership, and it now boasts almost 2000 local nature loving members. I even organised a group get-together at RSPB Ham Wall, which proved popular. Social media brings people together!

Greylake and the other wetland reserves on the Somerset Levels are nationally important habitats for teal. They're our smallest duck, and congregate in large numbers in autumn and winter, quite often associating with wigeon. A group of teal is called a spring, named after their ability to 'spring' suddenly into the air, vertically out of the water! They fly at great speed and twist and turn with amazing manoeuvrability, making them a particularly challenging duck to photograph in flight. I liked this photo of three teal in a line, a female flanked by two handsome males. You really can't appreciate how fast they were flying!

Some birds have featured more in this book than others. I'm better known for my pictures of the common birds, so it made sense to include a selection of my favourite shots of popular garden birds such as robins, blue tits and starlings. I love all birds, and I'll certainly try to see and photograph a rare bird if one turns up locally, but the common birds are always there, so give me countless opportunities to photograph them! It's difficult to put into words the joy I feel at taking pictures of all kinds of wild birds. I feel a charge of excitement go through me every time I pick my camera up and leave the house. Part of this is from travelling into the unknown. I don't know what I'll see and I don't know what I'll take a picture of, if anything!

These bickering starlings were at RSPB Greylake. It's amazing that such sociable birds squabble with each other so often! I've also noticed that they do not bully or bicker with smaller birds, even around food. It's only other starlings, at feeding time, that they take exception to!

Whilst writing this book, I've tried to keep all the personal recollections to those related to nature only. No room for other experiences, such as the time I embarrassed myself when I met Princess Diana, the time a ghost crept into bed with me, the time I almost killed myself with a rotovator in a strawberry field, the time I saved Bear Grylls' life (sort of), the time I won £4000 from a national newspaper, the time I told the great Stanley Baxter to get off a wall, or the time a guy, covered in blood, knocked on my van window, down a country lane in the middle of the night, begging me to get out and find his glasses, which he'd dropped somewhere in the road!

Maybe these stories will feature in my next book, or maybe they won't. The birds are far more interesting after all. A world without birds is a world I wouldn't want to live in. Luckily, I won't see that world, but there's a real chance my daughters, or my future grandchildren, will have to contemplate a bird-less existence, unless drastic measures to save the environment start now.

This photo is a very late entry into the book, in fact, it only just made it! Taken just a few days before the time of writing, it's quite an unusual picture, as most 'birds after bugs' pics are of the bird flying up to catch the fly, or chasing it horizontally. I was lucky enough to catch the moment the wagtail turned in mid-air, wings open, eyes looking down at its potential prey, which had dropped below it in a bid to escape its pursuer. I have a couple of more photos of the brief 'life or death' chase, but unfortunately, I'll never know if the wagtail was successful on this occasion, as both the fly and the bird disappeared from view before I could see the outcome of their mid-air duel.

I had been on my way back home from another local trip to RSPB Greylake, on what was an all too rare sunny autumn day. I never tire of photographing the small birds there, but my best shot of the day came as I stopped to photograph a buzzard on some hay bales near Westonzoyland Airfield, one of the oldest airfields in England, and a former RAF base during the 2nd World War. After the buzzard had flown off, I noticed this pied wagtail on top of a metal shed, waiting for passing flies.

Many years ago, I lived on a farm and nursery on the airfield with my family. We grew shrubs and vegetables, and had a paving yard, which was hard, heavy work. We also had a 'pick your own' strawberry field, and I used to sit up there in a caravan taking payment from the pickers. I used to stay on the edge of the field all day, listening to the wonderful song of the corn buntings on the wires across the main road.

Little did I know then, but I'd never see or hear them again. Westonzoyland Airfield was the last place in Somerset that these birds were able to cling on to survival. Once they were lost there, they were lost to the whole County. I wish I'd appreciated them more at the time, they're another example of once common farmland birds, driven to the brink by modern farming methods. I could cry with despair.

'Super Robin arrives to save the day, joining Super Tit in the fight against avian evil, the bird Avengers were born!'

This was the caption I gave this photo when I posted it on Twitter, a week before the time of writing. My followers love a character to root for and they decided that Super Robin just had to be in the book!

I have so much to thank my Twitter and Facebook followers for. It's purely thanks to them that the book you are now holding in your hands exists at all! I would never have had the confidence to even consider writing a book before, even though it had been a dream since I was a little boy.

I've been posting my nature pictures online for over 13 years, but it was only a year ago that I decided to make my own photography products available for people to buy. I always ask my Twitter followers for advice and pointers before I get new products printed. It's such a valuable source of research for me. For example, I asked them if it would be a good idea to get some postcards of my birds made. That idea was met with lots of positive comments, apart from one by the owner of a local card shop, suggesting greeting cards sell a lot better than postcards. Well I chanced it, and quickly sold hundreds of postcards! The aforementioned card shop owner was amazed, and when I said that I'd pop into her shop one day, she replied that she had to meet the person who could sell so many cards!

Well, a couple of weeks later I went to see her in her fantastically named shop, 'Jane Armour Trading', in Taunton, Somerset. She kindly went out and bought me a coffee, whilst I browsed her wonderful stock, which included cards from my friend, the talented artist Jackie Curtis. Jane told me that what I was doing was quite remarkable. From her many years experience of selling cards, ones with photos on never sell as well as ones featuring art. Photography is such a saturated market, she said.

I left her delightful shop feeling ten feet tall. She showed me such 'love and affection..'

Chiffchaff

The chiffchaff is a small warbler, weighing no more than 9 grams wet through! It's probably best identified by its song, where it helpfully belts out its name, over and over again. It's a monotonous, but very familiar sound in the countryside during spring and summer. They're almost identical to their close relative, the willow warbler, and their song is the best way to differentiate them. Of course, if they're not singing, this doesn't help, so then a decent view of their legs is important. Chiffchaffs have dark legs, willow warblers are pale.

My middle daughter, Erin Louise, has the rare distinction of having a pair of fighting chiffchaffs land on her head, during a family walk at Shapwick Heath in Somerset! I doubt very much that this has ever happened to anyone else before, anywhere, in the history of the world! Luckily for her, the combined weight of the bickering birds would have been no more than 18 grams, so no injury or headache was sustained. She did warble on about it for a few days after however.

I took this photo recently at RSPB Greylake. It was another case of being in the right place at the right time. It took me by surprise, I'd never seen a chiffchaff continually hover out in the open for such a long period of time before. I think it was looking for bugs on a wooden gate, and I gleefully took advantage of the unusual opportunity, and got a picture that has become a late, and the last, entry in this book!

I hope that through this little book I've been able to impart on you all at least a hint of my passion for our feathered friends. I've striven, both with pictures and words, to showcase just how truly beautiful and fascinating even the most common of British birds are, and that appreciating and capturing that beauty is not all about expensive equipment, technical know-how, or spending hours waiting around in a hide for something to present itself. It's more about getting outside, enjoying the wonderful green spaces around us, not looking for that 'one shot', but being in the moment and appreciating these wonderful creatures.